EATING FOR VICTORY

HEALTHY HOME FRONT COOKING ON WAR RATIONS

REPRODUCTIONS OF OFFICIAL SECOND WORLD WAR INSTRUCTION LEAFLETS

FOREWORD BY JILL NORMAN

First published in Great Britain in 2007 by
Michael O'Mara Books Limited
9 Lion Yard
Tremadoc Road
London SW4 7NQ

A CIP catalogue record for this book is available from the British Library

ISBN 978-1-84317-264-2

1 3 5 7 9 10 8 6 4 2

Designed by Design 23

Printed and bound in Great Britain by
Butler & Tanner Ltd, Frome

Many thanks to Stephen Jones and the staff at the National Archives in Kew
from whose archives the leaflets reproduced in this book were sourced.

CONTENTS

FOREWORD

Rationing in Britain during the Second World War was seen as a necessary evil, but the government at the time went to great lengths to ensure that everyone had enough to eat. They were determined, as the official leaflets reproduced in this book demonstrate, that the people in Britain should be fit to carry on the fight and for many this meant adopting a far healthier diet than they had ever enjoyed before. Even today we can learn a great deal about health and nutrition from the efforts that were made during the war years.

At the end of the First World War, the government took stock of the food problems faced during that period. This led to extensive technical investigations into food preparation, preservation, storage and transport, and to increased research into the scientific aspects of food and nutrition. During the great depression at the end of the 1920s, when unemployment exceeded two million, the poorest people could just about afford to buy sufficient calories to stay alive, but not to buy the milk, fruit and vegetables that would ensure they had sufficient protein, minerals and vitamins. In the 1930s a study organized by the British Medical Association showed that only the richest part of the population received a surplus of these basic dietary constituents; all the rest, some forty million people, were deficient to some extent, and four-and-a-half million were deficient in all constituents. Calcium deficiency was one of the biggest problems, which prompted the government to promote the drinking of milk in schools.

The outbreak of war in 1939 made it imperative to apply the findings of nutritional science to feeding the population, and plans

for rationing and distribution were drawn up, based on the experience of the Great War. The Ministry of Food was run very effectively by its scientific adviser, the nutritional biochemist Sir Jack Drummond, and the Minister, Lord Woolton, who had seen the effects of malnutrition and neglect in Liverpool and was determined to use his position to stamp them out. The two men set out to improve the nutritional content of the nation's diet. It was the first time modern theories of nutrition were applied to feeding a nation. Drummond's organizational flair, together with Woolton's determination to simplify rationing, confining it to goods whose supply could be guaranteed, led to a national food policy that promoted adequate nourishment and the economical use of foodstuffs.

Between 1940 and 1941, British agriculture was expected to supply about a third of the nation's food energy requirements, two thirds of the calcium, a third of the vitamin A, two fifths of the vitamin B1 and, as a result of increased potato production, all the necessary vitamin C. It was decided to increase home production of milk and vegetables and to increase supplies of imported dried and condensed milk, canned fatty fish and pulses, although imports of fruits, except oranges, were reduced as being wasteful of shipping resources.

It was, of course, essential to increase agricultural production to compensate for the loss of imports. Yet in spite of significant efforts, the energy value of home-produced food rose only from the pre-war level of 900 calories per head per day to 1200 (about forty per cent of the total) in 1943–44. The level of imports dropped to less than half the pre-war level, and became increasingly uncertain due to the threat from German submarines, which sank some 2,500 merchant ships during the course of the war. The emphasis for imported foods was on those with the highest energy values: oilseeds, oils and fats, canned meat, cheese, processed milk and boneless or compressed meat carcases (which made it hard for cooks to know what part of the animal they were dealing with). Sugar imports fell to about half their pre-war level in the years

1942–44. To cope with the reductions in the amount of wheat imported, more flour was extracted from the grain available. The extraction rate of national flour was raised to around eighty-five per cent, giving the population the nourishing wholemeal National Loaf (with a high vitamin B1 content), although many people did not find its greyish colour appetizing.

Unfamiliar foods such as dried eggs and dried skim milk were introduced, and it was necessary to teach the public how to use them.

Dried eggs were an invaluable invention of the food technologists, but they were particularly unpalatable. However much the advisers to the Ministry of Food tried to convince the public that a tablespoon of egg powder mixed with two tablespoons of water was just as good as a fresh egg, people knew it lacked the flavour and the texture. Dried eggs were best used in baking and puddings; scrambled dried eggs and omelettes lacked appeal. Many dairy herds were slaughtered so that pasture could be ploughed to grow food; this resulted in a shortage of milk, and the introduction of milk powder, which was more readily accepted. It was important, too, to explain how to get the maximum vitamin C from vegetables by cooking them conservatively or by eating raw salads.

This led to an extensive programme of cookery teaching and of education in nutrition, by means of leaflets of the kind reproduced here, books, posters, radio broadcasts and demonstrations. Some eighteen million people listened to the early morning five-minute BBC radio programme, *The Kitchen Front*. With the assistance of domestic science teachers, dieticians, school- meal organizers, hospital caterers, the Advice

Division of the Ministry of Food gave the public lasting guidance about the healthiest way to feed themselves and to make the best use of their rations.

Rationing was introduced in January 1940; butter, bacon and sugar were the first goods to be rationed, followed in March by meat and preserves, in July by tea, margarine and cooking fats, and in 1941 by cheese. Later, foods such as breakfast cereals, biscuits, canned fruit, condensed milk, sweets, chocolate and rice were added to the ration list. Milk and eggs were allocated, and there was also a points rationing scheme for buying non-perishable foods that were too scarce to ration. For these foods, everyone had 16 points per month, which was eventually increased to 20. At the end of the war, a severe global shortage of cereals led to flour, bread and cakes also being rationed; bread rationing lasted from July 1946 until July 1948. Some foods were de-rationed soon after the end of the war, but food rationing was not finally ended until 1954, when cheese, fats and meat came off ration and ration books became redundant.

Every man, woman and child had a ration book, and food prices were pegged at a standard rate so that poorer people could buy the food they needed. Everyone was entitled to the same amount, except that agricultural and manual workers were allowed extra cheese for their lunch boxes, pregnant women and children were allowed additional milk and eggs, and children under five were allowed orange juice, blackcurrant juice, rosehip syrup and cod liver oil, but only half the meat ration. Householders had to register with their local shops, which were allocated enough food for registered customers. The shopkeeper removed or crossed off the relevant coupons for each food when the customers presented their rations books at the till.

If you stayed in a hotel or boarding house you handed in your ration book, although you could eat in a restaurant without giving up rationing coupons. The maximum price of restaurant and café meals was fixed at five shillings (25p) and, of course, restaurateurs also had to contend with the constraints of rationing. The government set up British Restaurants, run by local committees as non-profit-making enterprises, often in church halls and similar premises. They were clean and spartan, more like works canteens than restaurants, but provided a nutritious meal for about 1s 6d (8p). In May 1941, 79 million midday meals a week were eaten in school dining rooms, canteens and subsidized restaurants. By the end of 1944, the figure had risen to 170 million.

Foods that were not rationed included offal, chicken, rabbit and game. Fish was not officially rationed, but it was hard to come by, and often expensive. Horsemeat was available; later on corned beef and Spam (luncheon meat) arrived in Britain, and by the beginning of 1945 whalemeat and snoek (a canned, strong-tasting fish) arrived from South Africa. Corned beef and Spam were adopted, but horse, whale and snoek were outside British food culture and never really accepted.

Alcohol and cigarettes were never rationed, but were in short supply; coffee was not rationed either, but at that time was consumed in much smaller quantities than it is now, and real coffee was certainly very hard to come by. In 1942 a typical week's ration was 4oz (100g) bacon, 1s 2d (6p) worth of meat, 2–4 oz (50-100g) cheese, 4 oz (100g) margarine, 8oz (225g) sugar, 2oz (50g) tea, 1 egg; 2–3 pints (1.2–1.8 litres) milk. Additional monthly entitlements were 1 packet of dried milk, 350g (12 oz) sweets, and every two months 1lb (450g) jam.

Before the war, some families had stockpiled canned and bottled goods but once rationing started, hoarding food became an offence punishable by a substantial fine or imprisonment. As the war went on, more and more foods vanished from the shops, and the queues got longer.

Vere Hodgson gave an account of living on the ration: 'Meat ration lasts for only three evening meals, ... that is Saturday, Sunday, Monday. Tuesday and Wednesday I cook a handful of rice, dodged up in some way with curry or cheese. But the cheese ration is so small there is little left. Thursday I have a pound of sausages. These make do for Thursday, Friday and part of Saturday ... All rather monotonous, but we are not hungry, and the authorities have done well for us, we consider.'[1]

At the beginning of the war, the government launched the Dig for Victory campaign, to encourage people to dig up their rose beds and herbaceous borders and plant vegetables instead.

All over the country gardens, parks, golf clubs, tennis courts, roadside verges, even window boxes became vegetable plots. Leaflets, similar to the cookery leaflets in this book, were distributed to promote vegetable growing. By 1943 it was estimated that over one million tons of vegetables were being grown in gardens and allotments, and many lawns had been turned into chicken runs. Generally, people living in the country were better off than those in the cities and large towns. They had more space for their vegetable growing, and access to mushrooms, berries and other wild foods, as well as sometimes being able to get butter, eggs and meat off ration. In some neighbourhoods pig clubs were established, the pig being fed from leftover scraps; some people kept goats for milk, and others bred rabbits.

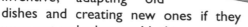

British cooks had to be inventive, adapting old dishes and creating new ones if they were not to be hungry. Nothing was wasted. Bacon rinds were put on joints and steaks to help make dripping, or fried till crisp and used to flavour a soup; apple peels were simmered in water till soft and strained so that the liquid could be substituted for lemon juice to provide pectin for jam making.

The leaflets distributed by the Ministry of Food fell into different categories: some gave helpful recipes to get the best from the rations, by making pies, stews and puddings, using up stale bread in stuffings to serve with meat; others concentrated on making healthy vegetable soups and salads, or suggesting different ways of preparing potatoes. Their high vitamin C content meant potatoes were a vital part of the diet; posters of 'Potato Pete' encouraged cooks to scrub potatoes instead of peeling them. Some leaflets explained new ingredients, like dried eggs, and how to reconstitute and use them; others on preserving or *What's Left in the Larder?* ensured nothing was wasted, and another set concentrated on nutritional aspects, like *Foods for Fitness* and *Your Vitamin ABC*.

The information in *Foods for Fitness* and *Your Vitamin ABC* is just as relevant today as it was sixty years ago, and the former ends with a salutary note that is worth heeding now: 'Appetite is a good guide to our needs of ... energy foods and, if we take more than we require, we generally store the surplus as fat.'

During the war, although there were privations and shortages, people generally had a good diet. When the war ended, it was found that the average food intake was much higher than when it began. This was mostly because many poor people had been too poor to feed themselves properly, but with virtually no unemployment and the rationing system, with its fixed prices, they ate better than in the past. School dinners, milk, orange juice and cod liver oil provided poor children with more nutritious food than they had had before. People at all levels of society took nutrition seriously and fed their families sensibly with the rations and whatever vegetables and fruit were available, and with less sugar and fewer sweet snacks there was less tooth decay. As a whole the population was slimmer and healthier than it is today; people ate less fat and sugar, less meat and many more vegetables.

Food writer Irene Veal dedicated her book, *Recipes of the 1940s,* published in 1943, to Lord Woolton, and wrote in her preface: 'Never before have the British people been so wisely fed or British women so sensibly interested in cooking.' *Eating for Victory* offers another record of recipes and nutritional advice that was used by thousands of people during the war, and still has relevance today. If you want to try out some of the recipes, you may need to use a little imagination to replace ingredients such as dried eggs that you may not easily be able to find in the shops, but there is a table of weights and measures at the back of the book if you are not familiar with some of the terms used during the 1940s. So, if you are feeling adventurous, why not rustle up a nutritious meal and see how you might have fared on wartime rations, eating for victory!

JILL NORMAN

---

1 Vere Hodgson *Few Eggs and No Oranges* 1976, entry for May 1944.

DRIED EGGS

The Ministry of Food dried egg is pure fresh egg with no additions, and nothing but the moisture taken away. It is pure egg, spray dried.

Eggs are a very highly concentrated form of food. They contain first-class body-building material. They also help us to resist colds and other infection because of their high protective properties.

Eggs are easily digested, and for this reason are especially good for children and invalids.

Dried eggs are just as good as fresh eggs, and should be used in the same way. They are very useful for main dishes. Here are some recipes for a variety of appetising dishes in place of meat, fish or cheese and which are particularly suitable for dried egg.

HOW TO RECONSTITUTE DRIED EGG

$$\left.\begin{array}{ll} 1 \text{ level tablespoonful egg powder} \\ 2 \quad\text{,,}\qquad\text{,,}\qquad\qquad\text{water} \end{array}\right\} \text{equals 1 egg.}$$

Methods.

1. Mix the egg and water and allow to stand for about five minutes until the powder has absorbed the moisture. Then work out any lumps with a wooden spoon, finally beating with a fork or whisk.

2. Mix egg to a smooth paste with half the water. Beat till lumps have been removed. Add the remaining water and beat again.

3. For plain cakes and puddings, batters, etc., the egg can be added dry and mixed with the other dry ingredients. When adding the liquid to the mixture an additional 2 tablespoons per dried egg used must be allowed.

USE AT ONCE.

After reconstituting the egg use at once. Do not reconstitute more egg than necessary for immediate use.

METHOD OF COOKING

Use in recipes exactly as fresh eggs, beating as usual before adding to other ingredients.

STORAGE

Keep the egg powder in a tin with a tight fitting lid, and store in a cool place. Do not keep dried egg in a refrigerator.

BACON AND EGG PIE

2 eggs (reconstituted);
2 rashers of grilled bacon;
8 oz. potato pastry;
2 oz. mashed potato;
Salt and pepper.

Method.—Beat the egg. Line a plate with half the pastry. Mix the egg, potato, salt and pepper, and chopped bacon together. Pour this mixture on to the plate, cover with the rest of the pastry. Bake in a moderate oven for ½ hour. Serve hot with vegetables or cold with salad. (Sufficient for 4.)

EGG CUTLETS

1½ lbs. mixed cooked vegetables (chopped finely);
1½ ozs. oatmeal;
4 dried eggs in powder form;
Salt and pepper.

Method.—Mix all ingredients together. Heat a little fat in frying-pan till smoking hot and fry spoonsful of the mixture till golden brown all over. Serve sprinkled with chopped parsley. (Sufficient for 4.)

OMELETTE

2 eggs (reconstituted);
½—¾ oz. margarine or fat;
Salt and pepper.

Method.—Beat the egg and salt and pepper. Heat fat in the pan, pour in the egg and work it with a fork in the usual manner. Fold over and serve immediately.

SPANISH OMELETTE
(Variation)

2 eggs (reconstituted);
8 ozs. grated mixed vegetables;
A small piece of chopped leek or parsley;
2 tablespoons water;
Salt and pepper;
1½ oz. margarine or dripping.

Method.—Beat the eggs. Heat the fat in a frying pan and fry the vegetables and leek until tender. Add the eggs, water and seasoning. Stir until the eggs are set, then shape into a crescent, and serve immediately. Or serve flat without folding. (Sufficient for 4.)

SCRAMBLED EGG

1 egg (reconstituted);
½ oz. fat;
1 tablespoon milk.
Salt and pepper.

Method.—Add the milk and seasoning to the reconstituted egg and beat lightly with a fork. Melt the fat in a saucepan, add the mixture and cook over a very low heat, stirring as little as possible until it just sets. Serve at once.

Note. To make this dish go further, diced cooked vegetables can be added.

MOCK FRIED EGG

1 egg (reconstituted) ;
2 slices wheatmeal bread ;
Salt and pepper.

Method.—Beat the egg. Cut holes from the centre of each slice of bread with a small scone cutter. Dip the slices quickly in water and then fry on one side until golden brown. Turn on to the other side, pour half the egg into the hole in each slice of bread, cook till the bread is brown on the underneath side. The bread cut from the centres can be fried and served with the slices.

MADEIRA CAKE

2 eggs (reconstituted or used dry - see method 3 page 1);
$\frac{1}{4}$ lb. national flour;
2$\frac{1}{2}$ ozs. margarine;
3 ozs. sugar;
2 level teaspoons baking powder;
A little milk :
Flavouring if liked.

Method.—Beat eggs. Cream margarine and sugar, add eggs one by one, beating thoroughly. Add flour, baking powder and flavouring. Bake in a moderate oven 1$\frac{1}{2}$—2 hours.

CAKE OR PUDDING MIXTURE

1 egg (reconstituted or used dry - see method 3 page 1) ;
4 ozs. national flour ;
2 ozs. sugar ;
2 ozs. fat ;
1 level teaspoon baking powder;
A little milk.

Method.—Beat egg. Cream fat and sugar, beat in egg, add the flour mixed with the baking powder. Mix to a soft consistency with a little milk. Spread in tin and bake for 15—20 minutes.

Note. This mixture can be steamed in a basin for 1 hour and served as a pudding with a jam or custard sauce. (Sufficient for 4.)

COQUET PUDDING

$\frac{1}{4}$ lb. potatoes ;
$1\frac{1}{2}$ ozs. margarine ;
$1\frac{1}{2}$ ozs. sugar ;
2 eggs (reconstituted or used dry - see page 1) ;
$\frac{1}{2}$ pint household milk ;
1 tablespoon dried fruit ;
or 1 tablespoon jam.

Method.—Cook and mash potatoes with margarine. Add sugar and eggs, beating well. Mix in milk and fruit and pour into a greased pie-dish. Bake in a moderate oven for 30 minutes. (Sufficient for 4.)

YORKSHIRE PUDDING

1 egg (reconstituted or used dry - see method 3 page 1) ;
4 ozs. national flour ;
$\frac{1}{2}$ pint of milk ;
Salt ;
1 knob dripping or fat.

Method.—Beat egg well. Mix flour and salt. Make a hole in the centre and put in the egg and sufficient milk to make a stiff mixture. Beat well, add the rest of the milk. Make the fat smoking hot in a baking tin and pour in the batter. Cook in a brisk oven for about 30 minutes.

Note. To this foundation recipe diced cooked vegetables and chopped cooked meat can be added. The addition of fresh or dried fruit makes an attractive sweet dish. The same mixture can be used for pancakes. Pour spoonfuls on to a piping hot greased pan or hotplate.

STEAMED CUSTARD

2 eggs (reconstituted) ;
$\frac{1}{2}$ pint of milk ;
Sugar ;
Flavouring.

Method.—Beat egg and sugar, add milk and flavouring ; pour into a greased cup or mould ; steam in a saucepan until set. (Sufficient for 2.)

BAKED CUSTARD

$1\frac{1}{2}$ egg (reconstituted) ;
$\frac{1}{2}$ pint of milk ;
Sugar ;
Flavouring.

Method.—Beat egg and sugar, add milk and flavouring, pour into a greased dish and bake till set in a slow oven.

Note. This can be baked in a pastry case and served as a custard flan. (Sufficient for 2.)

"ONE-POT" *Meals*

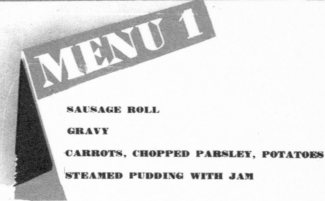

MENU 1

SAUSAGE ROLL

GRAVY

CARROTS, CHOPPED PARSLEY, POTATOES

STEAMED PUDDING WITH JAM

SAUSAGE ROLL

8 oz. sausagemeat

2 tablespoons finely chopped onion or leek

1 tablespoon chopped pickle

3 oz. breadcrumbs

Pinch of mixed herbs

Pinch of pepper

1½ teaspoons salt

2 tablespoons stock or milk

Mix all the ingredients together thoroughly. Turn into a greased tin. Cover with lid and steam 1½–2 hours.

UTENSILS REQUIRED

1 LARGE SAUCEPAN WITH A LID

2 8-OZ. COCOA TINS WITH LIDS

GRAVY

3 tablespoons flour
Pinch of pepper
½ pint vegetable water

1 meat cube
Gravy browning

Blend the flour and pepper with a little cold water, pour on the vegetable water
and return to the pan with the meat cube. Bring to the boil, stirring all the time
and boil for 5 minutes. Add gravy browning and salt if necessary.

STEAMED PUDDING WITH JAM

6 oz. plain flour and
3 teaspoons baking powder
or 6 oz. self-raising flour
Pinch of salt

1½ oz. margarine or cooking fat
1½ oz. sugar
Just over ¼ pint milk and water
2 tablespoons jam

Mix together the flour, baking powder if used, and salt. Rub in the margarine or
fat and add the sugar. Mix to a dropping consistency with milk and water. Put the
jam at the bottom of a greased tin and add the pudding mixture. Cover with lid
and steam for 1½—2 hours.

ALL QUANTITIES FOR 4 - ALL SPOONS LEVEL

METHOD ★

Method to have dinner ready by 1 p.m.

Preparation : Make up the roll, put into a tin and place the lid on.
Make the steamed pudding and put into a tin, put the lid on.
Prepare the vegetables.

11-0	Put the 2 tins into the saucepan with enough boiling water to come half-way up the tins. Put on the lid and keep the water boiling gently.
12-0	Add 2 teaspoons salt to the water and put 1 lb. carrots, cut in small chunks, in the pan round tins.
12-15	Put 1½ lb. potatoes in the pan with the carrots.
12-50	Dish up. Sprinkle carrots with coarsely chopped parsley. Keep hot while making gravy with the vegetable water.
1-0	Serve.

COOKING TIME 2 HOURS

MENU 2

HOT-POT

CABBAGE

MOCHA WHIP

HOT-POT

½ oz. dripping or cooking fat
2 oz. chopped onions
4 lamb chops
1 lb. potatoes, sliced thinly
8 oz. carrots, sliced
8 oz. turnips, sliced

Pinch of mixed herbs
2 teaspoons salt
¼ teaspoon pepper
½ pint water or stock
8 oz. finely shredded cabbage

Melt the dripping or fat and fry the onions and chops on both sides for about 5 minutes. Lift out the chops and put in the mixed vegetables, herbs, salt, pepper and liquid ; put back the chops on top. Cover the pan and simmer for 30 minutes. Add the cabbage and cook for a further 10-15 minutes.

MOCHA WHIP

8 tablespoons flour
3 oz. sugar

1 tablespoon cocoa
1 pint black coffee

Mix the dry ingredients to a smooth paste with a little of the liquid. Bring the remainder to the boil and pour on to the blended mixture. Return to the pan and stir until it boils. Boil gently for 5 minutes, stirring frequently. Leave to cool then whisk until light and frothy. Serve in four individual glasses.

METHOD ★★

Method to have dinner ready by 1 p.m.

12-0   Prepare the vegetables for the hot-pot.

12-10   Make the pudding.   (If more convenient the pudding may be made earlier in the day.)

12-20   Start the hot-pot. Prepare and shred the cabbage.

12-15   Add the finely shredded cabbage to hot-pot.

1-0   Dish up.

COOKING TIME 1 HOUR

MENU 3

BRAISED MEAT

POTATOES - MIXED ROOT VEGETABLES

WATERCRESS

SUMMER PUDDING AND CUSTARD

UTENSILS REQUIRED   LARGE SAUCEPAN WITH LID
                          BASIN FOR PUDDING

BRAISED MEAT

2 lb. stewing beef
1 oz. cooking fat or dripping
1½ lb. mixed root vegetables

2 teaspoons salt
¼ teaspoon pepper
½ pint stock or water

Roll the meat and tie securely or cut it into neat pieces. Heat the fat or dripping and brown the meat on both sides. Remove the meat from the pan, strain off any fat and add the vegetables. Add the seasoning and liquid, then place the meat on top of the vegetables, put on the lid and boil gently for 2 hours.

SUMMER PUDDING

8 oz. fresh fruit (red or black if possible)
1–2 oz. sugar

¼ pint water
5 oz. stale bread, cut ¼"–½" thick

Stew the fruit with the sugar and water until tender. Cut a round of bread to fit the bottom of a basin (1 pint size) and line the side with fingers of bread cut slightly wider at one end than the other. Fit the fingers of bread together so that no basin shows through. Half fill the basin with stewed fruit. Cover with a layer of scraps of bread left from cutting the round, etc. Add the remaining fruit and cover with a layer of bread. Pour the rest of the juice over all and cover the pudding with a weighted plate or saucer. Leave for at least two hours to cool and set. Turn out carefully and serve with custard.

N.B.—Very juicy fruit does not require any water for stewing. Bottled fruit may be used if fresh fruit is not available.

METHOD ★★★

Method to have dinner ready by 1 p.m.

Preparation : Make the pudding and leave to cool and set. Make the custard. Prepare the vegetables. (If more convenient the pudding and custard may be made earlier in the day).

11-0   Heat the fat in the saucepan, brown the meat on both sides ; remove the meat, add the vegetables, seasoning and stock, and place the meat on the vegetables.

12-25   Put 1½ lb. potatoes on to steam above or round the meat and other vegetables.

1-0   Dish up. Decorate the root vegetables with watercress.

COOKING TIME 2 HOURS

MENU 4

FISH STEW

COLE SLAW

SEMOLINA

MOULD

UTENSILS REQUIRED   1 SAUCEPAN   1 MOULD

FISH STEW

1 lb. white fish
8 oz. onions, sliced
8 oz. tomatoes, sliced
1½ lb. potatoes, peeled and cut into chunks

2 teaspoons salt
½ teaspoon pepper
¼ pint water
2 tablespoons flour

Remove any skin and bone from the fish and cut it into 1" cubes. Place in a pan with the vegetables, seasoning and water.   Simmer gently for 30 minutes.   Blend the flour with a little water and add to the stew, stirring all the time. Cook for 5 minutes, then serve in a hot dish.

COLE SLAW

8 oz. finely shredded cabbage heart
3 tablespoons finely chopped onion

About ¼ pint salad dressing

Shred the cabbage heart as fine as match sticks, mix with the onion and dressing and turn into a salad bowl. Chopped chives may be used instead of the onion or the bowl can be rubbed round with garlic before the cabbage is placed in it.

SEMOLINA MOULD

4 tablespoons semolina
2 tablespoons sugar
Pinch of salt

1 pint milk or fruit juice
Flavouring to taste

Mix the semolina, sugar, and salt to a smooth paste with a little of the cold liquid. Boil the remaining liquid and, when boiling, pour it on to the blended semolina. Mix well, return to the pan, stir until it boils and boil for 5 minutes. Flavour to taste and pour into a wetted mould. Leave to set. Serve with jam.

METHOD ★ ★ ★ ★

Method to have dinner ready by 1 p.m.

Preparation : Wash, peel and prepare the vegetables.

12-5   Make the semolina mould and put aside to cool. (If more convenient the pudding may be made earlier in the day.)

12-15   Make the fish stew.

12-25   Make the cole slaw.

1-0   Dish up.

COOKING TIME 55 MINUTES

MENU 5

SCOTCH BROTH

PILCHARD SALAD

STEAMED
CHOCOLATE
PUDDING

UTENSILS REQUIRED

1 LARGE SAUCEPAN WITH STEAMER TO FIT, 4 SMALL MOULDS OR CUPS FOR PUDDING

SCOTCH BROTH

1 oz. pearl barley
2 pints stock
2 teaspoons salt
¼ teaspoon pepper
6 tablespoons diced carrot

4 tablespoons diced turnip
2 tablespoons diced potato
2 tablespoons chopped onion
4 tablespoons shredded cabbage
1 tablespoon chopped parsley

Wash the barley and soak overnight in the water. Place in a pan with the seasoning and bring to the boil, add the carrot, turnip, potato and onion and boil for 40 minutes Add the cabbage and boil for 10 minutes. Add the parsley just before serving.

PILCHARD SALAD

4 pilchards
8 oz. apples, cubed (may be omitted if not available)
8 oz. cold cooked potatoes, cubed
2 tablespoons chopped parsley
1 tablespoon chopped leek or onion

2 tablespoons salad dressing
8 oz. finely shredded cabbage or other greens
Watercress
1 dozen radishes

Flake the fish and mix with the apples (if used), potatoes, 1 tablespoon parsley, leek or onion and salad dressing. Arrange the shredded greens on a dish, pile the fish mixture on top and decorate with the remaining parsley, watercress and radishes.

STEAMED CHOCOLATE PUDDING

5 oz. self-raising flour
or 5 oz. plain flour and
2½ teaspoons baking powder
1 tablespoon sugar

2 tablespoons cocoa
1 oz. margarine or cooking fat
2 tablespoons syrup
6 tablespoons milk and water

Mix the dry ingredients thoroughly and rub in the margarine or fat. Slightly warm the syrup and milk and water and add to the dry ingredients, beating until the consistency of batter. Pour into 4 small greased moulds or cups, cover with greased paper and steam for ½–¾ hour.

METHOD ★★★★★

Method to have dinner ready by 1 p.m.

Preparation : Prepare the salad ingredients and vegetables for the soup. Make the steamed pudding.

12-10 Begin making the soup.
12-15 Place the pudding in the steamer.
12-40 Add the vegetables to the soup.
12-50 Add the cabbage to the soup.
1-0   Dish up.

COOKING TIME 50 MINUTES

MENU 6

CHEESE POTATOES
STEAMED CELERY
RAW VEGETABLE SALAD
SUET CRUST PUDDING

UTENSILS REQUIRED

LARGE SAUCEPAN AND STEAMER
BASIN FOR PUDDING

CHEESE POTATOES

2 lb. potatoes
4 oz. grated cheese
2 teaspoons salt

Pinch of pepper
½ teaspoon dry mustard
4 tablespoons milk

Cook the potatoes until soft, drain and mash well. Beat in the cheese, seasonings and milk. Serve immediately.

RAW VEGETABLE SALAD

10 tablespoons grated raw carrot
8 tablespoons grated raw turnip
4 tablespoons grated raw parsnip
2 tablespoons finely chopped onion
2 tablespoons finely chopped celery

3 tablespoons coarsely chopped watercress
2 tablespoons salad dressing
Sprigs of watercress to decorate

Mix the vegetables together and moisten with the salad dressing. Turn into a salad bowl and decorate with sprigs of watercress.

SUET CRUST PUDDING

6 oz. plain flour
2 teaspoons baking powder
¼ teaspoon salt
1–1½ oz. suet or cooking fat

1 oz. grated raw potato
Water to mix (about 4 tablespoons)
1 lb. fresh fruit
1½–2 oz. sugar

Mix the flour, baking powder and salt together. Add the suet, or rub in the fat, and potato and mix to a soft dough with water. Roll out two-thirds of the dough and line a one-pint basin. Fill with fruit and sugar and moisten the edges of the lining. Roll the remaining dough to the size of the top of the basin and cover the fruit. Press the edges of dough together, cover with greased paper and steam for 1½ hours.

METHOD ★★★★★★★

Method to have dinner ready by 1 p.m.

Preparation : Make the pudding and prepare the vegetables.

11.45   Put the pudding on to steam in the steamer, and put the celery on to steam round the pudding basin.

12.15   Put the potatoes in saucepan to cook in the water below the steamer. Prepare the raw vegetable salad.

12.45   Remove the potatoes from the pan. Mix with the other ingredients as in recipe.

1.0   Dish up.

COOKING TIME 1½ HOURS

MENU 7

BACON HOT-POT

SHREDDED CABBAGE

DUMPLINGS WITH SYRUP

UTENSILS REQUIRED

PAN AND STEAMER, BASIN OR CAKE TIN FOR HOT-POT

BACON HOT-POT

1½ lb. potatoes, cut in thin slices
2 oz. onions, finely chopped
3 oz. bacon, finely chopped
2 tablespoons chopped parsley

2–3 teaspoons salt
½ teaspoon pepper
¼ pint stock
8 oz. shredded cabbage

Grease a cake tin or pudding basin. Arrange layers of potatoes, onion, bacon and parsley in it, seasoning each layer. Add the stock, cover with a plate or a piece of greased paper and steam for 1½ hours. 15 minutes before serving arrange cabbage round tin or basin to steam.

DUMPLINGS

4 oz. plain flour and
2 teaspoons baking powder
or 4 oz. self-raising flour

Pinch of salt
1 oz. suet
Water to mix

Mix all the dry ingredients together and add enough water to make a soft dough. Divide into 8 portions and roll into dumplings. Cook in boiling water for 10–15 minutes. Strain and serve with syrup.

METHOD ★★★★★★★

Method to have dinner ready by 1 p.m.

Preparation : Prepare the vegetables and other ingredients for the hot-pot.

11-30 Put the hot-pot on to cook in the steamer.

11-45 Put the cabbage in the water with 2 teaspoons salt. Make the dumplings.

12-55 Lift off the steamer, dish the cabbage and put fresh water in the sauce-pan. Bring to the boil and add the dumplings which will cook while the first course is being eaten.

1-0 Dish up the hot-pot.

COOKING TIME 1½ HOURS

Issued by the Ministry of Food 27-9-46—51-2569

Making the most of the MEAT

This leaflet explains four simple ways of treating meat to make sure it will be tender.

SLOW ROASTING

Ordinary roasting methods are only suitable for the following cuts of meat : *Beef*, rump, sirloin, fore ribs, wing ribs and best chine ; *Lamb* and *Veal*, leg, loin and shoulder ; *Pork*, leg and loin. Slow roasting is suitable for any of these joints and also for the following : *Beef*, top side, middle ribs or brisket ; *Lamb* and *Veal*, neck or breast ; *Pork*, spare ribs.

METHOD Put the meat in a roasting pan in the usual way, adding a little dripping if the joint is very lean. Cook in a slow to moderate oven (325°F–350°F) that is, about the same heat as for a large fruit cake. The time needed will depend on the weight and thickness of the meat but the average is about 45 minutes per lb. for pork, beef and lamb, and 50 minutes per lb. for veal. This is for joints weighing more than 3 lb. Smaller joints need even longer per lb. With slow roasting there is no need to baste during cooking unless the joint is very lean.

If Yorkshire pudding and roast potatoes are to make part of the meal, the oven will have to be made hotter for the last half hour of cooking. The potatoes should either first be boiled until half cooked, that is " parboiled," and then browned quickly, or they may be baked with the meat and browned off at the end of cooking. Less dripping is used if the potatoes are cooked in a separate baking tin, so if you have room in the oven put a little dripping from the joint in a tin, roll the potatoes in this, and put them in the hottest part of the oven.

When the meat is cooked, make the gravy in the usual way, being sure to use vegetable water or other stock to give a good flavour.

BRAISING

Braising can be used for large or small joints, as well as for chops or pieces of steak. Meat cooked in this way is always tender and has a lovely flavour from the vegetables which are cooked with it.

Suitable cuts of meat for braising are : *Beef*, top side, skirt, brisket or middle bs ; *Lamb*, middle neck, scrag or breast ; *Pork*, spare ribs ; *Veal*, neck, breast or scrag.

GENERAL METHOD Braising can be done either on top of the stove or in the oven, but first the meat must be fried. So if you are going to use an oven casserole which will not stand frying heat the meat should be browned in a frying pan and transferred to the casserole for the rest of the cooking.

1 Trim off all surplus fat. This can be rendered down later for dripping. If too much fat is left on the joint the cooked meat will be greasy and unappetising.

2 Prepare enough vegetables to make a thick layer (1 to 2 inches) on the bottom of the pan. The vegetables may be diced or sliced. Suitable vegetables are onions, carrots, turnips, celery, peas, tomatoes, swedes and parsnips.

3 Heat enough fat to cover the bottom of the pan and when it is very hot fry the meat on all sides until it is a good brown colour. Lift it out and fry the vegetables lightly. This is not essential but improves the flavour. Drain off all surplus fat.

4 Season the vegetables, adding salt, pepper, herbs and spices to taste. Add about 1 inch of stock or water (not enough to cover the vegetables) and place the meat on top. It should always be above the level of the liquid.

5 Put on the lid and cook very slowly until the meat is tender. The time to allow for chops and small pieces of meat is about ¾ hour ; for joints allow 40 to 45 minutes to the lb. A thin piece of meat needs less time than a thick piece of the same weight.

6 Lift the meat on to a serving dish and carve in the usual way. The nicest way of serving is to put the carved slices overlapping on the dish, decorate with the vegetables and pour the gravy over the meat. If preferred, the gravy may be thickened with flour and coloured with gravy browning before serving. Any meat left over may be treated in the same way as meat from a cold roast joint.

BRAISED STUFFED BREAST OF LAMB OR VEAL

1 large or 2 small breasts of lamb or 1 breast of veal — Stuffing (see recipes back page) — 1 oz. fat or dripping for frying — 1 lb. mixed vegetables, diced — 2 teaspoons salt — Pinch of pepper — ½ pint vegetable stock or water.

Bone the breast and remove any surplus fat. Spread with a layer of stuffing and roll up. Tie lightly with string or tape. Make any remaining stuffing into balls. Then follow the general directions for braising given above. Fry or bake the stuffing balls separately and serve them round the meat and vegetables.

BRAISED SPARE RIBS OF PORK

2–3 *lb.* spare ribs
1 *oz. fat or dripping for frying*
2 *medium onions, sliced*
1 *medium apple, chopped*
8 *oz. carrot and turnip, diced*
4 *oz. tomatoes, fresh, sliced or bottled or 2 or 3 sticks celery, chopped*
½ *teaspoon ground mace*
½ *teaspoon ground nutmeg*
1 *teaspoon salt*
Pinch of pepper
1 *pint stock or water*
Follow the general braising method already given.

BRAISED LAMB CHOPS

4 chops
½ oz. fat or dripping for frying
3 bacon rinds
mixed vegetables, diced
8 tomatoes, sliced

Flavourings :—1 clove, 1 blade mace, 2 or 3 peppercorns, tiny sprig of thyme, 1 or 2 leaves of mint
1 teaspoon of salt
Pinch of pepper
¼—½ pint stock or water

Trim all the surplus fat from the chops. Heat the fat or dripping and bacon rinds in a pan and fry the chops until well browned on both sides. Remove from the pan and pour off the fat. Place the vegetables in the pan with the tomatoes, flavourings, seasoning and stock or water. Lay the chops on the vegetables, cover the pan with a lid. Cook very gently for about ¾ hour. Remove the bacon rinds and serve the chops on a hot dish with the vegetables and gravy.

STEWING

Stewed meat is served under many different names, including brown or white stew, casserole, hot pot and curry. Sometimes the meat is fried before stewing but this varies with the recipe. Any kind of meat can be used, beef, veal, lamb, mutton, pork, game and offal. Any vegetables in season are suitable for flavouring.

TIPS FOR MAKING GOOD STEWS

1 Cut the meat in convenient sized pieces for serving, removing all surplus fat and save it to render down for dripping. Fat left on the meat makes a stew greasy and unappetising.
2 Do not use more liquid than necessary to moisten the meat and provide just enough gravy for serving. Adding too much liquid is one of the most common causes of a tasteless stew.
3 A stew must not be allowed to boil. It must be simmered, that is, the surface of the liquid should be quite still or at the most, only an occasional bubble should appear. If you cannot regulate the heat on the top of the stove to make it slow enough put the stew in a double boiler or in a basin over a pan of gently boiling water. Another excellent way of cooking a stew is to put it in a casserole or other dish with a lid and cook it in a slow oven, using the same heat as for a milk pudding.
4 Flavour well with vegetables, including onions, leeks or garlic, herbs, salt and pepper. A little sugar added to a stew improves the flavour. Vinegar or lemon juice helps to make meat more tender. If vinegar from the pickle bottle is used extra flavour is added as well. Use about 1 tablespoon for a stew for 4 people.
5 Long, slow cooking improves the flavour. Stews need from 1½ to 3 hours or until the meat is tender.

WHITE STEW

1 lb. scrag end or middle neck of lamb or ¾ lb. pork or veal
8 oz. onions
4 oz. carrot
3 oz. turnip
1 bay leaf

¾ pint stock or water
3 teaspoons salt
¼ teaspoon pepper
4 tablespoons flour
1 tablespoon chopped parsley

Cut the meat into suitable sized pieces for serving and put into a saucepan with the peeled and sliced vegetables, stock or water and seasoning. Simmer for 1½–2 hours, stirring occasionally. Mix the flour to a smooth paste with a little cold water. Add some of the hot gravy from the stew, mix well and return to the saucepan and stir until it boils. Boil for 5 minutes. Serve hot, sprinkled with chopped parsley.

BROWN STEW

1 lb. stewing meat (beef, lamb, veal, or pork)
4 tablespoons flour
3 teaspoons salt
¼ teaspoon pepper

1 oz. cooking fat or dripping
8 oz. onions, sliced
8 oz. root vegetables, sliced
A small piece of bay leaf
¾ pint water

ALL SPOONS LEVEL   ALL RECIPES FOR FOUR

Cut the meat into pieces (about 1 inch cubes) and roll in the flour and seasoning ur well coated. Melt the fat or dripping in a saucepan and fry the meat until a good brown colo Add the vegetables to the meat with the bay leaf and water. Simmer for 1½-2 hours, or ur tender.

MEAT CURRY

1 small onion	½ teaspoon dry mustard
1 medium sized apple	¾ pint stock or water
1½ oz. dripping	1 teaspoon sugar
¾-1 lb. beef or lamb	1 tablespoon chutney or vinegar
1½ tablespoons curry powder	1 tablespoon marmalade
4 tablespoons flour	1 teaspoon black treacle or syrup
	2 teaspoons salt

Chop the onion and the apple finely and fry in the melted dripping. Add the meat in 1 inch cubes and fry lightly. Remove the meat from the frying pan and work in the cu powder, flour, and dry mustard. Cook for 2-3 minutes, add the liquid gradually and bri to the boil, stirring all the time. Add the sugar, chutney, marmalade, black treacle or syr and salt. Replace the meat and simmer for 1-1½ hours, or until tender. In place of rice se either macaroni, barley or potatoes with the curry.

DUMPLINGS

To add bulk to the stew—

4 oz. plain flour and	¼ teaspoon salt
2 teaspoons baking powder or	Milk to mix, about 3-4 tablespoons
4 oz. self-raising flour	

Mix the dry ingredients together. Add enough milk to mix to a soft dough. Cut mixture into 8 portions and shape roughly into dumplings with the hands. Drop into stew and cook for 10-15 minutes with the lid on.

Recipes using **MINCED** *or finely chopped meat*

Mincing or chopping breaks up the tough, coarse fibres of the meat and makes it eas to chew. In this way tough cuts of meat can be made palatable without long slow cookir It is also a good way of distributing a little meat evenly as in the " Savoury Meat Puddin

MINCE-IN-THE-HOLE

4 oz. minced meat, fresh or cooked (beef, pork, lamb, or veal)
1 leek, chopped finely
2 teaspoons mixed herbs
1 teaspoon salt
Pinch of pepper
½ oz. cooking fat or dripping

BATTER :
4 oz. flour
1 to 2 eggs
½ teaspoon salt
Pinch of pepper
½ pint milk or water (approx.)

Mix the mince, leek, herbs ar seasoning together. Form into bal Melt the fat in a baking pan, put in th meat balls and put in the oven to hea Mix the flour, eggs, salt and pepper to thick batter with some of the liquid, be well, add more liquid to make a th batter and beat again. Pour this over tl balls and bake in a hot oven for 30— minutes.

HAMBURGERS

8 oz. minced beef
4 oz. stale bread, soaked and squeezed
Pinch of herbs
2 teaspoons salt
½ teaspoon pepper
¼ teaspoon mustard
4 teaspoons Worcester sauce
2 tablespoons chopped onion
1 egg (optional)

Mix all the ingredients together and form into eight rounds. Fry in shallow fat for 15 minutes or until cooked in the middle. Put a large saucepan lid over the frying pan during cooking as this conserves the heat. Serve with potatoes and watercress or raw salad.

HAMBURGERS IN BROWN SAUCE

Hamburger recipe as above.

SAUCE :
2 oz. dripping
1 small onion, chopped
1½ oz. flour
1 pint water or stock
Gravy browning
½ teaspoon salt

¼ teaspoon pepper
1 teaspoon vinegar
1 teaspoon chutney
1 teaspoon sugar
2 tablespoons diced carrot
2 tablespoons diced potato

Melt the dripping and fry the hamburgers until brown but not cooked through. Remove from the pan. Fry the onion until brown. Add the flour and mix well. Add the liquid gradually, stirring until the sauce boils. Add the other ingredients and the hamburgers, cover and simmer for 15-20 minutes.

SAVOURY MEAT PUDDING

PASTRY :
8 oz. plain flour
2 teaspoons baking powder
½ teaspoon salt
1 oz. suet or cooking fat
1 oz. grated raw potato
Water to mix

FILLING :
8 oz. minced or chopped beef, pork, lamb or veal
3 tablespoons flour
1 lb. diced vegetables
3 tablespoons chopped leek or onion
1-2 teaspoons salt
Pinch of pepper
½ pint stock
Gravy browning

Mix the flour, baking powder and salt. Rub in the fat or suet and mix in the grated potato. Mix to a stiff dough with cold water. Line the basin with ¾ of the pastry. Mix the meat with the flour. Arrange layers of the vegetables, leek, meat and seasoning in the basin. Add the stock in which a little gravy browning has been mixed. Roll out the rest of the pastry to fit the top. Press the edges together. Cover with greased paper and steam for 2½-3 hours.

Stuffing can stretch the meat in two ways. By adding to the bulk and by adding a body building food such as the egg in the recipe below. The stuffing can either be cooked in the meat or formed into balls to cook round the joint or in a separate pan. Both slow roasting and braising are good ways of cooking a stuffed joint.

MINT STUFFING

6 oz. stale bread, soaked and squeezed
4 tablespoons chopped onion
6–8 tablespoons chopped mint
1–2 tablespoons vinegar
1 tablespoon sugar
2 teaspoons salt
2 teaspoons bacon fat
1 egg

Mix all the ingredients together and use to stuff lamb or mutton.

FORCEMEAT STUFFING

6 oz. stale bread, soaked and squeezed
2 tablespoons chopped parsley
1 teaspoon mixed herbs
2 teaspoons salt
½ teaspoon pepper
½ oz. dripping, cooking fat, or bacon fat

Mix together the bread, parsley, herbs, and seasoning. Melt the dripping or fat, and add to the dry ingredients. Mix thoroughly. Use as required.

APPLE AND CELERY STUFFING

6 oz. stale bread, soaked and squeezed
3 oz. chopped onion
6 oz. chopped celery
3 oz. chopped apple
2 teaspoons salt
½ teaspoon pepper
2 teaspoons sage
Water to mix

Bind the ingredients together with a little water and use as required.

RHUBARB AND RAISIN STUFFING

6 oz. stale crusts, soaked and squeezed
½ oz. suet, dripping or bacon fat
2–3 oz. chopped rhubarb
2 tablespoons chopped raisins
2 teaspoons salt
Pinch of pepper
1 teaspoon thyme

Mix all the ingredients together. If using dripping or bacon fat melt this before adding it to the dry ingredients. Use for stuffing pork, lamb or veal.

THE Ministry of Food has compiled the " ABC of Cookery" which gives suggestions and methods for cooking and preparing food. Obtainable from H.M. Stationery Office or through any Bookseller. Price 1/- or 1/2 by post.

10 MENUS FOR HIGH TEAS AND SUPPERS

HIGH TEAS AND SUPPERS

A good high tea or supper should include either a raw salad or a correctly cooked vegetable dish and one of the body-building foods such as cheese, egg, bacon, meat or fish. These can be supplemented with a vegetable body-builder such as peas, beans, lentils or oatmeal.

The ten menus suggested here all contain body-building and protective foods with bread, cake or scones as "fillers." For recipes for salads and soups ask for the salad and soup leaflets.

MENU I

VEGETABLE SOUP
★ BEEF & LETTUCE SALAD WITH MUSTARD SAUCE
BREAD & MARGARINE

BEEF & LETTUCE SALAD WITH MUSTARD SAUCE

4 tablespoons flour	1 tablespoon vinegar
1 tablespoon mustard	4 oz. corned beef
1 teaspoon salt	1 medium lettuce
½ teaspoon pepper	A few radishes and cooked
½ pint water	peas to garnish
1 tablespoon finely chopped onion	

Mix the flour, mustard, salt and pepper to a smooth cream with a little of the water, and add the onion. Boil the rest of the water and pour on to the blended mixture. Return to the pan, bring to the boil and boil gently for 5 minutes. Beat in the vinegar and allow to cool. Flake the corned beef, shred the heart of the lettuce and mix them with the cold sauce. Line a bowl with the outside leaves of the lettuce and pile the filling in the centre. Garnish with slices of radish and cooked peas.

MENU 2

★ SALMON CROQUETTES
RAW VEGETABLE SALAD
BREAD, MARGARINE & JAM

SALMON CROQUETTES

3 tablespoons flour	½ pint stock or milk and water
¼ teaspoon ground mace or nutmeg	2 teaspoons vinegar
¼ teaspoon pepper	4 oz. household salmon, mashed
1 teaspoon salt	Browned breadcrumbs

Blend the flour, spice and seasoning with a little of the cold liquid. Bring the remainder to the boil, pour on to the blended flour and mix well. Return to the pan, bring to the boil, stirring all the time, and boil gently for five minutes. Beat in the vinegar and fish and turn on to a wetted plate. When cold and firm, divide into four or eight portions and form into sausage shapes. Roll in browned breadcrumbs and grill for a few minutes until golden brown. Serve hot or cold with mixed salad.

N.B. If liked, pilchards or sardines may be used in place of the salmon.

MENU 3

★ WELSH WONDER
WATERCRESS SANDWICHES
PLAIN CAKE

WELSH WONDER

8 large leeks	6 tablespoons grated cheese
Salt and pepper	

Cut the leeks in half lengthwise and wash well. Cook in a very little boiling salted water. When tender, drain well, keeping the vegetable water for soup or gravy. Place in a baking dish; sprinkle with salt and pepper and grated cheese. Place under the grill to melt the cheese.

NOTE.—Other vegetables suitable for cooking this way are: cauliflower, potatoes, artichokes, celery, cabbage or a mixture of cooked vegetables in season.

MENU 4

★ SALMON SAVOURY
WATERCRESS & BEETROOT SALAD
BREAD, MARGARINE, JAM OR SWEET SPREAD

SALMON SAVOURY

4 tablespoons plain flour	½ teaspoon mixed herbs
¼ pint water	1 teaspoon vinegar
4 oz. canned salmon	Salt and pepper

Mix flour with a little of the water, bring remainder of water to boiling point, add to flour paste and allow to boil for 5 minutes. Then add salmon herbs, vinegar and seasoning to taste. Turn on to slices of toast and place under a grill for 2 minutes. Serve immediately.

MENU 5

★ MACARONI CHEESE
TOMATOES OR WATERCRESS
JAM TART

MACARONI CHEESE

5 oz. macaroni
3 tablespoons flour
½ pint milk
½ pint macaroni water

½ teaspoon made mustard
¼ teaspoon pepper
4 oz. grated cheese

Cook the macaroni in boiling salted water until tender—about 20-30 minutes. Drain well and keep hot. Blend the flour with a little of the cold milk. Boil the rest of the milk with the macaroni water and pour on to the blended flour. Return the mixture to the saucepan and bring to the boil, stirring all the time. Boil gently for five minutes. Add the seasoning with two-thirds of the grated cheese and the macaroni. Mix well, turn into a greased pie-dish and sprinkle the remainder of the cheese on top. Brown under the grill.

MENU 6

★ CREAMED SARDINE PIE
GREEN SALAD
BREAD, MARGARINE & JAM

CREAMED SARDINE PIE

3 tablespoons flour
½ pint milk and water
1 teaspoon salt
Pinch of pepper
Pinch of ground mace or
    nutmeg

1 teaspoon vinegar
1 can sardines in oil
    (4½ oz. size)
6 oz. short pastry
A little milk

Blend the flour with the milk, bring to the boil, stirring all the time, and boil gently for 5 minutes. Add the seasoning, mace or nutmeg and vinegar. Mix well and beat in the sardines with the oil. Line a 6-inch flan ring or sandwich tin with half the pastry, add the mixture and cover with the remaining pastry. Brush the top with a little milk and bake in a hot oven for 25-30 minutes. Serve hot or cold with a green salad.

MENU 7

★ FISH & POTATO PANCAKE
COLE SLAW
ROCK BUNS

FISH AND POTATO PANCAKE

1 medium-sized onion,
    finely chopped
½ oz. dripping or fat
¾ lb. potatoes, cooked and
    sliced
1 lb. cod or any white fish,
    cooked and flaked

1 teaspoon vinegar
1 teaspoon salt
Pepper
Chopped parsley

Fry the onion in the dripping or fat until tender. Add the potatoes and fish and fry until brown. Sprinkle over the vinegar, salt, pepper and parsley. Serve hot.

QUANTITIES FOR 4 PERSONS - ALL SPOONS ARE LEVEL

MENU 8

★ SARDINES & CHEESE SAUCE
RAW VEGETABLE SALAD
BREAD, MARGARINE & JAM

SARDINES ON TOAST WITH CHEESE SAUCE

1 *tin sardines*	4 *tablespoons grated cheese*
4 *slices of toast*	*Pinch of mustard*
½ *oz. margarine*	*Salt and pepper*
2 *tablespoons plain flour*	*Parsley to garnish*
¼ *pint milk*	

Arrange the sardines on toast, then make a thick white sauce with margarine, flour and milk, and allow to boil. Draw pan away from heat and stir in gradually the cheese. Return to heat and, stirring all the time, just bring to boil. Season well, coat sardines with the sauce. Decorate with a little chopped parsley.

MENU 9

★ SPLIT PEA SOUP
CHEESE & SALAD SANDWICHES
PLAIN CAKE

SPLIT PEA SOUP

5 *oz. split peas*	½ *teaspoon celery salt*
2 *pints water*	1½ *teaspoons salt*
1 *onion or leek, chopped*	¼-½ *teaspoon pepper*
1-2 *bacon rinds*	1 *tablespoon flour*
½ *oz. dripping or fat*	¼ *pint milk*

Wash the peas and soak overnight in the water. Fry the onion or leek and the bacon rinds in the dripping or fat for a few minutes. Add the seasonings, peas and water. Cover the pan with a lid and bring to the boil. Boil gently until the peas are tender, about 1½-2 hours. Remove the bacon rinds. Blend the flour with the milk, stir into the soup and bring to the boil, stirring all the time. Boil for 5 minutes. Serve hot.

MENU 10

★ LEEK & POTATO SOUP
PILCHARD & CABBAGE SANDWICHES
DROP SCONES OR PANCAKES

LEEK AND POTATO SOUP

4 *medium sized leeks*	*Salt*
½ *oz. fat or dripping*	4 *tablespoons household milk*
3 *medium sized potatoes, sliced*	(dry)
1 *quart water or vegetable stock*	*Chopped parsley*

Cut the leeks in half lengthwise, and wash well; chop finely. Melt the fat in a saucepan and fry the leeks gently for 15 minutes without browning; keep the lid on. Add the potatoes, ¾ of the stock and cook until the potatoes are tender. Mix the milk to a smooth paste with the remaining stock and add to the soup. Bring to the boil and sprinkle with chopped parsley just before serving.

POTATOES

THERE is no vegetable more useful than the homely potato
It is a valuable yet cheap source of energy, and one of the foods
that help to protect us from ill-health. It contains vitamin
C as do oranges and 1-lb. of potatoes daily will give half
the amount of this vitamin needed to prevent against fatigue
and help fight infection.

So don't think of potatoes merely as something to serve with
the meat. They can be much more than that. A stuffed baked
potato can be a course in itself. Potatoes can be used, too, in
soups, salads, pastry, savoury supper dishes and even biscuits,
as the following recipes show.

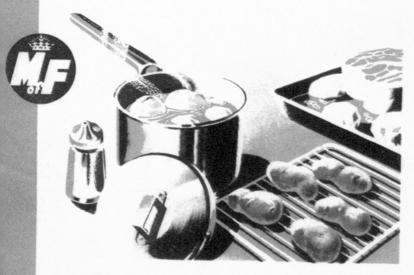

HINTS ON COOKING & SERVING POTATOES

ONE ➤ Cook them in their skins whenever possible.

TWO ➤ If you must peel them, peel thinly.

THREE ➤ After peeling, cook at once.
Avoid soaking in water if possible.

FOUR ➤ Serve potatoes immediately as keeping them hot destroys some of their protective qualities.

FIVE ➤ Use potato water for making soups and gravies.

SIX ➤ Potatoes left after a meal should be kept in a cool place and used for making pastry, pancakes, scones, potato salad or for thickening soups.

BOILED POTATOES

Allow 1½ to 2 lb. for 4 people

Scrub the potatoes, and put into boiling salted water using just enough water to cover.

Cook with the lid on. Keep the water boiling, but not too rapidly or the potatoes will break up and become mushy. When tender, drain carefully. Shake the potatoes gently in the saucepan over a low heat for a minute or two. This dries the potatoes and leaves them deliciously floury. Serve at once.

BAKED POTATOES

Scrub the potatoes and prick them. Place in a hot oven and bake until tender. This method can be used when cooking the rest of the dinner in the oven, so saving the "top heat." Alternatively place the potatoes in hot cinders under the fire. They take about 45 minutes, but the time varies with the oven heat and the size of the potatoes. To test when a baked potato is cooked squeeze it gently in a cloth. If soft it is ready to serve. Prick well again to allow steam to escape and make the inside floury.

N.B. If the potatoes are baked too slowly they will be soggy instead of floury.

FISH

ALL RECIPES

BAKED STUFFED POTATOES

4 medium sized potatoes (approximately 1 lb.)

4 oz. cooked minced meat
¼ pint brown sauce

1 teaspoon sauce
1 teaspoon salt

Pinch of pepper

Bake the potatoes whole without removing the skin. Cut a slice from the top. Take out the centre, mash well and mix with the rest of the ingredients. Pile back into the potato case and re-heat for a minute or two under the grill or in the oven. Serve hot.

ALTERNATIVE FILLINGS

1   4 oz. flaked cooked fish
¼ pint white sauce

1 teaspoon salt
Pinch of pepper

2   3 oz. grated cheese
2 tablespoons chopped parsley

Pinch of pepper
2 tablespoons milk

3   4 oz. chopped cooked vegetables
¼ pint white sauce

2 tablespoons parsley
1 teaspoon salt

Pinch of pepper

4   1 oz. fried chopped bacon
3 oz. fried chopped onion

2 tablespoons chopped parsley
1 teaspoon salt

Pinch of pepper

5   4 oz. cooked sausage meat
1 tablespoon chopped parsley

1 teaspoon salt
Pinch of pepper

SAUSAGE

BACON

VEGETABLES

MEAT

FOR FOUR

MASHED POTATOES
1½-3 lb. for 4 people

Cook the potatoes by baking or boiling, remove from the skins and beat well with a little hot milk, or margarine, if these can be spared. Add salt and fresh coarsely chopped parsley, just before serving.

ROAST POTATOES
With fat

Prepare potatoes as for boiling. Place in a baking tin with a little fat and roast in a moderate or hot oven till golden brown and cooked right through. If meat is being roasted the potatoes may be cooked in the tin under or round the meat, but less fat is required if they are cooked separately.

ROAST POTATOES
Without fat

1 *pint water*	2 *lb. potatoes*
	1 *dessertspoon salt*

Peel the potatoes thinly and put into a roasting tin with the water, and salt. There should be enough room for them to lie comfortably without touching, and there should be enough water to half fill the roasting tin. Put the tin into a hot oven and bake for 1½ hours. The water evaporates and leaves shiny golden balls with floury insides.

POTATO SOUP

1½ *lb. potatoes*	¼ *pint milk, fresh, household or evaporated*
1 *stick celery, or a small onion, or a little leek*	2 *teaspoons salt*
	Pinch of pepper
1¾ *pints vegetable water or water*	2 *tablespoons chopped parsley*

Scrub and slice the potatoes and celery. Place in boiling salted water. Cook with the lid on until quite soft. Rub through a sieve. Add the milk and re-heat, but do not re-boil. Season well. Sprinkle coarsely chopped parsley over just before serving.

ALL SPOONS LEVEL

POTATO AND WATERCRESS SOUP

12 oz. potatoes
8 oz. watercress
½ oz. margarine or dripping

3 tablespoons flour
1 pint milk, or milk and water
Salt and pepper to taste

Cook the potatoes and watercress in ½ pint salted water until tender. Rub the cooked vegetables through a sieve and keep hot. Melt the margarine or dripping and stir in the flour. Mix until smooth. Add the milk or milk and water and stir until boiling. Boil for 5 minutes. Then add the vegetable puree, mix well and season to taste.

POTATO SALAD

Boil 1 lb. potatoes in their skins (extra can be done at dinner time). Peel and cut into dice. Add a little chopped onion. While still warm bind together with salad dressing. When cold, sprinkle with chopped parsley.

POTATO AND BACON CAKES

1 lb. cooked potatoes
6 tablespoons chopped onion
1½-3 oz. bacon
2 teaspoons meat or vegetable extract

½-1 teaspoon salt
Pinch of pepper
Milk and breadcrumbs for coating

Mash the potatoes well while still hot. Chop the bacon. Fry the bacon and then the onion till both are golden brown. Add to the mashed potato with the extract, salt and pepper. Mix well together and form into 8 cakes. Coat with milk and breadcrumbs and bake in a moderately hot oven till firm.

IRISH POTATO CAKES

8 oz. mashed potatoes
1 teaspoon salt
Pinch of pepper

½ oz. melted margarine
1-2 oz. flour

Mix the potato, salt, pepper, melted margarine and enough flour to make a stiff dough. Roll out to about ¼ inch thick and cut in 8 pieces. Cook on a hot plate or in a greased frying pan, browning them on both sides. Spread with margarine or sandwich fillings. They make a good breakfast dish if fried in the bacon fat.

POTATO AND CHEESE FLAN

6 oz. short crust pastry

FILLING

8 oz. cooked cubed potato	Pinch of pepper
3 oz. grated cheese	½ oz. flour
3 tablespoons grated celery	¼ pint milk
3 tablespoons grated onion	Breadcrumbs
1-2 teaspoons salt	

} white sauce

Line a 7 inch flan ring or sandwich tin with the pastry. Mix the potato, cheese, celery, onion and seasoning well together. Make the white sauce by blending the ½ oz. of flour with ¼ pint milk and stir until it boils. Boil for a few minutes. Add the sauce to the other ingredients. Place the mixture in the flan case. Sprinkle with breadcrumbs and bake in a moderately hot oven for 25-30 minutes.

POTATO STEW

½ oz. fat	2 lb. potatoes
4 rashers bacon, chopped	½ teaspoon herbs
4 tablespoons chopped onion	2 teaspoons salt
2 tablespoons flour	Pinch of pepper
1 pint of stock	Chopped parsley
2 tablespoons vinegar	

Melt the fat, and fry the bacon and onion for few minutes, add the flour and mix well. Add the stock and vinegar, and stir until boiling. Vegetable stock may be used, or water and meat extract. Peel and quarter the potatoes and add with the herbs, salt and pepper, cover and cook gently until the potatoes are tender, about 40 minutes. Sprinkle with chopped parsley.

POTATOES IN CURRY SAUCE

2 lb. potatoes	½ teaspoon mixed herbs
½ oz. fat	2 cloves
1 onion, chopped	Pinch of cinnamon and nutmeg
1 medium sized apple, chopped	1 teaspoon sweet pickle
1 small tomato	or 1 oz. sultanas
1 dessertspoon curry powder	1 teaspoon vinegar
2 tablespoons flour	1 teaspoon sugar
½ pint of stock or	2 teaspoons salt
meat extract and water	

Boil the potatoes and keep warm. Make the fat hot in a pan, put in the chopped onion and fruit and fry lightly without browning. Add the curry powder and flour, mix well, add the stock gradually and the rest of the ingredients. Boil gently for 5 minutes, stirring frequently, and adding a little water to make up to ½ pint. Pour over the potatoes and serve at once.

ONION AND CHEESE SUPPER DISH

½ oz. dripping or cooking fat
4 oz. finely chopped onion
2 oz. grated cheese
2 tablespoons chopped parsley

6-8 oz. mashed potato
½-1 teaspoon salt
Pinch of pepper

Melt the dripping or cooking fat in a saucepan, fry the onion till golden brown and tender, add 2/3rds of the cheese, the parsley and seasoned mashed potato. Mix well together over the heat till the mixture is warmed through. It may then either be put into a dish with the remainder of the cheese sprinkled on top and grilled or placed on four slices of toast and finished in the same way. Serve very hot with vegetables or salad.

SAVOURY POTATO SANDWICH SPREAD

Any of the fillings given for stuffed potatoes, mixed with an equal quantity of mashed potato, can be used for savoury sandwiches.

SAVOURY POTATO BISCUITS

2 oz. margarine
3 oz. plain flour
3 oz. cooked mashed potato
6 tablespoons grated cheese

1½ teaspoons salt
Pinch of cayenne
or black pepper

Rub the margarine into the flour. Add the potato, cheese and seasoning and work to a stiff dough. Roll out thinly, cut into shapes and bake in a moderate oven, 15-20 minutes. This quantity makes 24 3-inch biscuits.

POTATO PASTRY

8 oz. plain flour
½ teaspoon salt
2 oz. fat
4 oz. mashed potatoes

Mix the flour and the salt. Cream the fat and the potato, add the flour and a little water if necessary, to form a rather stiff dough. This pastry is very good used as a crust on meat pies or as a case for savoury flans. It is advisable to eat it fairly soon after baking as it becomes very dry if re-heated.

VEG.

MEAT

OR FOUR

PLAIN OR SWEET BISCUITS

4 oz. *plain flour*
4 oz. *rolled oats*
   or barley kernels
1-2 *teaspoons salt*

3 oz. *margarine*
4 oz. *cold mashed potatoes*
2 oz. *sugar (sweet biscuits*
   only)

Mix the flour, rolled oats or barley kernels and the salt. Rub in the margarine and then knead in the mashed potato. Continue kneading until the whole is a very stiff dough. No liquid should be used. Roll out until only 1/8 inch thick and cut into biscuits. The mixture makes about 3 dozen. Place on baking tins and bake in a slow oven until crisp but not brown, about 15-25 minutes. Cool on cake racks or in any way which will let the air circulate around them to make sure they will stay crisp.

SWEET BISCUITS

Add only a pinch of salt and the sugar to the other dry ingredients. Mix as before.

The Ministry of Food has compiled the A B C of Cookery, which gives suggestions for cooking and preparing food. Obtainable from H.M. Stationery Office. Price 1s. 0d. or by post 1s. 2d.

Issued by the Ministry of Food
Revised and Reprinted October, 1946

51-2622

64108210
Ppt. L.

FOODS FOR
FITNESS

AN A.B.C. OF CHOOSING FOODS

BODY BUILDING FOODS

Our bodies need raw material for building and growth and this can be obtained only from the food we eat. To build well we need the right foods.

An expectant mother is building a new body and children are enlarging their bodies by growing; both obviously have a special need for good quality building materials. But even for grown-ups body-building substance is still needed for maintenance and repair.

BONES AND TEETH—the foundation.

We need Calcium—to make our bones and teeth hard and strong. Vitamin D is necessary for fixing the calcium in the bones.

We find Calcium—in milk and cheese, which are our richest natural sources, and in smaller quantities in vegetables. It is now added to National Flour and hence to National Bread—to make sure that no one is short of this valuable nutrient.

FLESH AND MUSCLE

We need Protein—because our muscles are made largely of this body-building substance. Protein is necessary for life and is found in all living things.

We find Protein—In animal foods—meat, poultry, fish and in foods providing the essentials of growth for young animals, e.g. milk and eggs. Cheese which is made from milk is also a good source of protein.

—In vegetable foods such as peas, beans, lentils and other vegetables, cereals and nuts. These are not as good as, but will supplement, the animal protein which is harder to get. The resulting combination can be as good value as animal protein taken alone and, to-day, we must " stretch " the animal foods available by serving them with vegetable foods.

BLOOD—the transport system.

  Carries food and oxygen to all parts of the body.

We need Iron—for healthy red blood and vitality.

We find Iron—in strongly coloured foods, egg yolks, liver, meat, dark green vegetables, dried fruit and in many cereals such as flour and oatmeal.

PROTECTIVE FOODS

No matter how well built, the human body must be protected against ill health and disease by the right food. The " protective " parts of food—the vitamins—help to do this.

VITAMIN A

We need vitamin A—for growth, for the health of the throat, lungs, skin and eyes, and to enable us to adapt the sight to dim light.

We find vitamin A—in fish liver oils, liver, butter and other dairy produce, carrots and green leafy vegetables. In the U.K. it is now added to margarine.

VITAMIN D

We need vitamin D—to fix the calcium in growing bones and teeth in order to make them strong and healthy.

We find vitamin D—in fish liver oils, fatty fish, butter, the creamy part of milk, egg yolk. This vitamin, too, is added to our margarine.

Vitamin D is also formed by the action of sun on our skin and it is sometimes called the " sunshine vitamin."

THE VITAMIN B COMPLEX

We need the Vitamin B complex—for a healthy digestive system, a healthy nervous system and to help us in maintaining a good appetite.

We find the Vitamin B complex—in the outer layer and germ of the cereal grains, milk, national flour and bread, yeast, liver, pork, bacon and potatoes. It is also found in smaller quantities in many other foodstuffs.

VITAMIN C—the health and beauty vitamin.

We need vitamin C—for a clear skin, bright eyes and strong tissues. It is easy to go short of vitamin C if we do not plan and prepare our meals carefully.

We find vitamin C—in fruits and vegetables, especially green leafy vegetables, potatoes, citrus fruits, tomatoes, rose hip syrup and blackcurrant syrup.

Fruits and vegetables—the principal source of vitamin C in the diet—are bulky foods and unsuitable for the very young baby. Expectant mothers and babies are given orange juice because of its vitamin C content. Remember that vitamin C is easily destroyed by light, heat and by solution in cooking water. So, in your cooking, use fresh vegetables, cook quickly in a small amount of boiling water and serve immediately.

ENERGY FOODS

We need energy—to live and to work. The human body, like any engine, needs fuel. Our fuel is food. The harder we work physically and the harder we play, the more fuel we need; but we need some fuel just to live even when we are resting or sleeping.

We obtain energy—from all foods, but foods which contain a high proportion of fat, starch or sugar supply the most. Fat is a concentrated source of fuel or energy and without it a meal is not very satisfying. Starchy foods are good fillers and sugars and jams, too, give us energy.

Appetite is a good guide to our needs of these energy foods and, if we take more than we require, we generally store the surplus as fat.

GOOD FOOD
leads to
GOOD HEALTH

It is very important that we should understand the part that food plays in our lives and so be able to choose an adequate diet from the foods that are available.

During the last ten years, priority rationing schemes in this country have assured to particular sections of the community adequate supplies of the food known to be necessary to them. For example, expectant and nursing mothers and young children, whose need of milk far surpasses that of the average adult, have allocations of milk sufficient to meet their needs.

People have always realized that food was necessary for life and growth and they knew that certain foods pleased them and satisfied their appetite better than others ; but only quite recently has science taught us the function of food and the part that it plays in promoting good health.

Foods may be divided into three main groups according to the work they do. They are responsible for Building hard bones, muscle tissue and the blood supply: for Protecting the body against ill health and providing resistance to disease ; and for supplying fuel, the source of our Energy.

HOW TO PLAN YOUR MEALS

Well planned meals are important for the health of adults and children alike. One of the essentials of good health is adequate and well balanced feeding. As far as possible, every meal should contain some of the main building, protective and energy foods.

Consider a typical British tea or supper which might include fish, bacon, sausage or an egg. These are *Building foods* and can be served with vegetables or salad and perhaps also with potatoes and National Bread and butter which are *Protective foods* and help to supply vitamins. The bread and butter are good *Energy foods* too but the meal may also include further energy foods such as a sweet or cake or pastry. All your meals should follow this basic pattern.

SOME RULES FOR HEALTHY FEEDING

1. *Eat all your share of the Building foods*—supplement the animal foods meat, milk, cheese, eggs and fish by serving them with cereals, peas, beans, lentils or nuts.

2. *Eat plenty of fruit and vegetables*—We depend on these important foods for some of our vitamins and our diet would be incomplete without them. Eat potatoes and other vegetables daily.

3. *Fill up with Energy foods*—Cakes, buns, pastry, sugar, jam and bread are cheaper than most other foods — so be careful that in order to cut down on expense, you do not neglect to eat your builders and protectors.

Use Energy foods to satisfy your appetite after taking your share of 1 and 2.

51-1641 B.B.Ltd.

CHEESE

Cheese is an A.1 food because :—

It is an excellent body-builder, better than meat for building firm muscles. It builds strong bones and teeth, too. Therefore it is invaluable for growing children. Plenty of cheese in childhood means less dental troubles in later life.

It is a concentrated energy-giving food, especially suitable for heavy workers, as it gives a large amount of energy in small bulk. It contains a high proportion of fat and so gives a feeling of satisfaction after a meal.

It is also a valuable protective food, guarding against infection and helping to prevent certain forms of night blindness.

Cheese is such an important food it deserves a place of its own at meal-times. Use it as a main dish and not as an afterthought to a meal already containing meat or fish. Used in this way cheese can be made to help out the meat ration.

Cheese is not indigestible, even for children of 18 months, if eaten uncooked and grated.

How to keep Cheese.—Wrap it in a margarine or butter paper, hang in a piece of muslin in a cool, airy place. This hardens the cheese and makes it more economical in use. Use the rind for flavouring sauces, etc., but remember to remove it before serving the dish.

One of the easiest and pleasantest ways of serving cheese is with a green salad—this with potatoes is a perfect meal.

BREAKFAST DISHES

Tomato Cheese Savoury

4 tomatoes or 1 lb. cooked mixed vegetables.
1 lb. mashed potatoes.
3 oz. grated cheese.
Salt and pepper.

Method.—Cut tomatoes into slices or dice the cooked vegetables and place on a bed of mashed potatoes. Sprinkle with grated cheese, salt and pepper. Put under the grill until cheese has melted and browned. Serve hot.

Oatmeal Cheese Rarebit

(for one person)

1 oz. grated cheese.
½ oz. toasted oatmeal.
1 oz. flour.
¼–½ lb. mashed potatoes.
¼ pint water. Salt and pepper.
1 teaspoonful coarsely chopped parsley.

Method.—Mix flour with enough water to make a smooth paste. Boil the remaining water and add the flour paste, boiling for one minute. Add the cheese, oatmeal and seasoning, stir well and cook for a minute or two longer. Pour on to a flat bed of mashed potato and place under grill until brown. Sprinkle with parsley before serving.

MAIN MEALS

Vegetable Pie with Cheese and Oatmeal Crust

1½ lbs. cooked, mixed vegetables.
2 tablespoonfuls chopped parlsey.
½ pint stock or water.
2 oz. oatmeal. 4 oz. flour.
2 oz. mashed potato. ⎫
1 oz. fat. 2 oz. cheese. ⎬ Pastry.
Water to mix. Salt. ⎭

Method.—Place cooked vegetables in a pie-dish and sprinkle with coarsely chopped parsley. Add vegetable water and seasoning. To make the pastry, cream fat and potato together. Mix grated cheese, oatmeal, flour and salt and stir into it the creamed fat and potato. Mix to a stiff dough with water. Roll out the pastry, cover the pie and bake in a moderate oven for 30 minutes. Serve with baked jacket potatoes and greens.

Cheese Savoury

> 1 egg (i.e. 1 level tablespoonful of dried egg,
> 2 tablespoons of water).
> ½ pint milk, household milk or vegetable stock.
> 1 breakfast cup or 4 oz. breadcrumbs.
> 4 oz. grated cheese.
> Salt, pepper and mustard.

Method.—Reconstitute the egg and beat up with the milk. Add the other ingredients. Pour into a greased dish and bake for 20 minutes in a moderate oven until brown and set. Serve with baked jacket potatoes, mashed swedes and watercress.

Potato Jane

> 2 lbs. potatoes.　　　　　　　4 oz. grated cheese.
> 2 oz. breadcrumbs or oatmeal.
> ½ chopped leek.　　　　　　　1 sliced carrot.
> ½–¾ pint milk and water.　　　Salt and pepper.

Method.—Put a layer of sliced potato in a fireproof dish. Sprinkle with some of the leek, carrot, crumbs or oatmeal, cheese and seasoning. Fill dish with alternate layers, finishing with a layer of mixed cheese and crumbs, or oatmeal. Pour over the milk, cover with a lid or greased paper and bake in a moderate oven for ¾–1 hour or steam for 1–1½ hours. Serve with mashed carrots and swedes, sprinkled with coarsely chopped parsley.

Cheese Omelette

> 4 reconstituted eggs (4 level tablespoons
> dried egg, 8 tablespoons water).
> Salt and pepper.　　　2 oz. grated cheese.　　　Fat.

Method.—Beat eggs with seasoning. Heat sufficient fat in a pan to grease the bottom, rub the surplus fat round the sides of the pan. Pour in ¼ of the egg mixture, to cover the bottom, and shake well, using a fork to loosen the sides. When the eggs are set sprinkle with cheese and fold in half. Serve on to a hot plate and sprinkle with parsley or garnish with watercress or shredded raw cabbage. Repeat this process, making four omelettes in all.

SUPPER DISHES

Cheese Pancake

> 4 oz. flour.
> 2 oz. cooked mashed potato.
> 2 oz. grated cheese.
> 1½ gills milk and water.
> 1 teaspoonful baking powder.
> Salt and pepper.
> Pinch mixed herbs.

Method.—Mix the flour, mashed potato and liquid to make a batter, add baking powder and cheese. Melt fat in a frying pan and when smoking hot pour in sufficient batter to cover the bottom of the pan. Fry pancakes to a golden brown on each side.

If liked, this mixture can be made into drop scones, using a girdle, greased hot plate or frying pan.

Vegetable au Gratin

3 breakfast cups diced cooked vegetables.
1 breakfast cup cooked white or coloured beans.
1 small piece chopped leek.
3 oz. grated cheese.

Sauce

4 oz. flour.
½ pint vegetable liquid.
½ pint milk.

Method.—Mix the flour to a smooth paste with some of the liquid. Bring the rest of the liquid to the boil and pour over blended flour. Return quickly to the pan and cook for 5 minutes, stirring all the time. Add cooked vegetables and half the cheese. Pour into a fire-proof dish. Sprinkle with remainder of the cheese. Grill until brown, or brown at the top of the oven if the oven is in use.

Cheese Frizzles

4 tablespoons medium or coarse oatmeal.
2 tablespoons flour.
4 tablespoons grated cheese.
2 teaspoons baking powder.
Salt and pepper.
A little water to mix.
Fat for frying.

Method.—Mix all dry ingredients together except the baking powder. Add enough cold water to mix to a stiff batter. Just before using add the baking powder. Melt a little fat in a frying pan and when smoking hot drop spoonfuls of the mixture into hot fat. Fry till golden brown on both sides.

Cheese with Fish

Sprinkle some grated cheese over fish when baking it in the oven. This lends quite a new and subtle flavour to the fish.

Cheese Pudding

2 eggs (reconstituted).
½ pint milk.
2–3 oz. grated cheese.
1 teacupful of breadcrumbs.
Salt and pepper, mustard.

Method.—Beat the eggs. Boil the milk, stir in the crumbs and remove from the fire. Add cheese, salt, pepper, mustard and beaten eggs. Pour into a dish and bake or grill till brown.

CHEESE IN SANDWICHES

Cheese Fondant Filling

4 oz. cheese, finely grated.
1 tablespoon dried milk,
1 tablespoon water.
2 tablespoons coarsely chopped parsley.
1 teaspoonful chopped pickle or chutney.
Seasoning.
Few drops of Worcester sauce if liked.

Method.—Blend all ingredients together and season well. The mixture should be quite soft.

How to FRY

MINISTRY OF FOOD

MoF

LEAFLET

No. 25

Fats suitable for frying

A good frying fat should be free from moisture, which makes it splutter when heated and it should have what is known as a high "smoking temperature." When fat is heated it first of all melts, and then bubbles if there is any moisture in it. The bubbling is caused by the water being turned to steam and forced out of the fat. When it has finished bubbling the surface is still and presently a faint blue haze rises from the surface. If the fat is heated beyond this temperature it smokes and burns and is spoilt for further frying. A good frying fat is one which can be heated to a high temperature (not less than 360°F.) before it smokes and burns that is, it has a high smoking temperature. This is important because the fat must be hot enough to form a coating quickly on the outside of the food. This coating protects the food from becoming greasy.

Vegetable oils generally have a high smoking temperature and this is why they are commonly used for frying. A mixture of half beef and half mutton dripping also makes a good frying fat. Margarine and butter are not suitable for general frying purposes, although butter is good for omelettes and cooking vegetables. Pure lard is a good frying fat and some cooking fats are suitable for deep fat frying, others can only be used for shallow frying.

How to clarify fat

Clarifying means cleaning. Frying fat must be clean, as dirty fat burns readily and will quickly spoil. Frying fat should always be strained after use to remove any particles of food. Dripping which is mixed with gravy or specks of food must be clarified as follows before it is suitable for frying.

1 Put the fat in a saucepan and cover with water, but not with the lid.

2 Bring to the boil and pour it into a clean basin. If a very large quantity of fat is being clarified, strain the fat through fine muslin.

3 Leave until cold, when the fat will form a hard lid on top of the water and any impurities will be in the water or on the bottom of the fat.

4 Lift off the cake of fat, turn it upside down and scrape the bottom clean.

5 If the fat is to be used for cakes, pastry, puddings or spreads it may be used at this stage, but if it is wanted for frying or to be kept for some time the water must be removed.

6 Melt the fat in a saucepan and heat until it stops bubbling. This means that all the water has been driven off.

N.B. If the fat has a strong flavour, cook a raw sliced potato in it at stage 6. When the potato is brown, and the fat has stopped bubbling, strain into a clean dry basin. The potato absorbs flavours.

How to prepare food for frying

Many foods need a coating of either batter, egg and breadcrumbs or flour and milk. This coating sets when the food goes into hot fat and protects the inside from becoming greasy. Some foods form their own coating, but may have batter or egg and breadcrumbs added for variety in flavour and appearance. Foods for which a coating is not essential are meat, fish, raw potatoes, bacon, sausages and doughnuts.

Foods which must be coated are all mixtures using cooked potatoes, for example, rissoles, fish cakes, etc., croquettes or other mixtures of cooked food combined with a thick sauce; and fruit and cooked vegetables which are generally coated in an egg and flour batter and called "fritters."

Coating food for frying

Be sure the food is quite dry or the coating will not stick. It is often a help to dip the food in flour before putting it in the coating mixture.

EGG AND BREADCRUMBS

1 Dip the prepared food in beaten egg and make sure the whole surface is covered. Then dip in breadcrumbs, brown or white, and pat well to make the crumbs stick. Use fine crumbs as coarse crumbs fall off during frying and make the fat dirty.

THIN BATTER AND BREADCRUMBS

2 Make a batter of 1 tablespoon flour and 2 tablespoons milk and/or water. Dip rissoles, fish cakes, etc., in this, then roll in breadcrumbs. Enough for 4 rissoles or 4 pieces of fish.

FLOUR AND MILK OR EGG

3 Dip the prepared food in seasoned flour, then in milk or egg, and then in flour again. This coating is suitable for food which is to be fried in shallow fat.

COATING BATTER

4 Use a batter thick enough to coat the food evenly. It may be made of seasoned flour and water or a thick pancake mixture (see recipes).

SHALLOW or dry FRYING

This is cooking food in a frying pan with only enough fat to cover the bottom of the pan.

1 A heavy frying pan gives the best results.

2 Use clean fat, free from moisture as water in the fat makes it splutter when heated (see Stage 6, "How to clarify fat").

3 Use enough fat to cover the bottom of the pan.

4 Have the fat very hot before adding the food. It should be heated until a very faint blue smoke rises from the surface.

5 Bacon and oily fish such as herrings or sprats may be fried without any additional fat. Heat the pan before adding the food. With bacon let the rashers overlap so that only the fat parts touch the pan.

CLEANING FRYING PANS

Always wash well after use. To make the surface very smooth for omelettes and pancakes put in some ordinary cooking salt and rub well with a piece of paper.

DEEP FAT FRYING

1 Use a deep, heavy pan, as there must be room for enough fat to cover the food but at the same time the pan should be only half full. This is because when food is added to hot fat it bubbles violently and may boil over if the pan is too shallow. A deep pan gives better results than a wide one. Many pans sold for deep fat frying are much too wide and shallow to be satisfactory. An ordinary saucepan is quite good provided it is of thick metal.

2 A frying basket is a help in lowering food gently into hot fat and in lifting it all out together, but it is not essential. A perforated spoon or ladle is suitable. Food which is coated with batter should not be placed directly on the hot wires of the frying basket or the batter will stick to the wire. The basket should not fit the pan tightly or it will jam when heated.

3 Heat the fat gently. When it stops bubbling and a very faint blue haze rises it is hot enough to use.

The following is a useful test: Cut a 1-inch cube of stale bread and drop into the fat. If it browns in 1 minute, the fat is hot enough for frying. If the fat smokes it is burning and will be spoilt.

If a thermometer is available the following are the correct fat temperatures for frying:—

Food	Temperature	Time required for Cooking
Croquettes and fish cakes	390°F.	1 minute
Chops, coated with egg and crumbs	360-400°F.	5-8 minutes
Doughnuts	360°F.	5-8 minutes
Fritters	370°F.	3-5 minutes
Fish fillets	370°F.	4-6 minutes
Fish, small whole	370°F.	3-5 minutes
Potato chips	370-390°F.	4-8 minutes

4 Do not try to fry too much food at once as this reduces the temperature of the fat and the food will not cook properly.

5 Fried food should be drained on absorbent paper before serving.

6 When frying is finished strain the fat and keep for further use. If more fat is needed next time, fresh fat may be added.

RECIPES

Frying cooked potatoes

Cut cold boiled potatoes in slices ½-inch thick and fry brown on both sides in very hot shallow fat. Drain well and serve sprinkled with salt and chopped parsley.

Pancake batter

4 oz. plain flour
1 to 2 eggs, fresh or dried
Pinch of salt

Approx. ½ pint of milk
or milk and water
Fat for frying

Mix the flour and salt. Add the egg and sufficient milk to make a thick batter. Beat well and add more milk to make it the consistency of thin cream. Put the batter in a jug. Use just enough fat to grease the bottom of the pan, but have pan and fat very hot. Pour in a very thin layer of batter. When the underside is brown, loosen the edges and toss or turn it over. Turn it out on to paper covered with a thin layer of sugar and roll it up.

Batter for coating fish

Use the pancake recipe but add less milk so that the batter is thick enough to coat the fish well. Usually about ⅛ pint of milk is sufficient. Dip the fish in seasoned flour and then in the batter. Half the pancake recipe is enough for 4-6 pieces of fish.

Eggless batter FOR COATING FISH

2 oz. flour   ⅛ pint milk and/or water   Pinch of salt

Mix flour and salt to a batter with the liquid and use to coat food for frying. Enough for 4-6 pieces of fish.

Cheese and vegetable cutlets

4 oz. grated cheese
8 oz. mashed potato
4 oz. cooked peas
2 carrots, finely grated
1 onion, chopped finely

4 level tablespoons flour
Salt and pepper
Thin batter for coating
Browned breadcrumbs

Mix together the cheese, vegetables and flour and season well. Form into 8 cutlets, dip in batter, and coat with browned breadcrumbs. Fry in a little hot fat until golden brown on both sides.

Fish cakes

½ lb. cooked fish
½ lb. mashed potatoes
1 onion, finely chopped
1 tablespoon chopped parsley
Pepper

Few drops vinegar
1 dried egg reconstituted for
coating or thin eggless batter
Breadcrumbs

Flake fish finely. Mix all ingredients together, form into cakes, dip in reconstituted egg or thin eggless batter and breadcrumbs, and fry in deep or shallow fat.

NOTE   If preferred, the onion may be fried or boiled before adding it to the other ingredients.

Chip potatoes

Choose large potatoes, scrub and peel them. Cut potatoes into ⅜-inch slices lengthwise and then cut again lengthwise to form long strips. If the chips are not to be cooked immediately cover them with cold water to prevent browning. Drain and dry very thoroughly on a clean cloth and fry in very hot fat. Deep fat is best for these, although they can be cooked in shallow fat.

FRITTERS

Batter recipe

4 oz. flour
Pinch of salt

1 egg, fresh or dried
Approx. ¼ pint milk and water

Mix the flour and salt to a thick batter with the egg and milk and water. Beat well and use as required,

N.B.—This recipe can be made without egg but 2 level teaspoons baking powder should be added to the flour.

Celery and cheese fritters

Add a pinch of mustard and pepper when making the batter and increase the salt to 1 level teaspoon. Stir into the batter 3 medium stalks of celery, chopped in small pieces, and 2-3 oz. grated cheese. Fry in spoonfuls in a little hot fat until golden brown on both sides.

Fish or meat fritters

Add a pinch of pepper to the batter and increase the salt to 1 level teaspoon. Stir in 6 oz. flaked fish or chopped cooked meat and fry as above. Slices of cooked meat may be fried in the same way as Apple Fritters.

Fruit fritters

Stir 2-4 oz. chopped dried fruit into the batter and fry as above. If liked, sprinkle with a little sugar before serving.

Apple fritters

Dip fresh apple rings into the batter and fry until golden brown and the apple is cooked.

Note

The methods described in this leaflet are demonstrated in the film, "How to Fry," made by the Ministry of Information for the Ministry of Food and the Ministry of Education.

Issued by the Ministry of Food
March, 1946

Printed for H.M.S.O. by Ppt. L.

6493503

Puddings

All quantities for 4

STEAMED PUDDINGS

Plain Steamed Pudding

8 oz. plain flour	2 oz. sugar
A pinch of salt	Milk, or milk and water to
4 level teaspoons baking powder	mix (just over ¼ pint)
2 oz. fat	2 dried eggs, dry

Mix together flour, salt, baking powder and dried egg. Rub in the fat until the mixture resembles breadcrumbs. Add sugar, and enough liquid to make the mixture a dropping consistency. Turn into a greased 6 in. basin and steam for 1 hour.

VARIATIONS OF PLAIN STEAMED PUDDING

FRUIT PUDDING. Plain steamed pudding, with 2—3 oz. dried fruit added with the sugar.

SPICE PUDDING. Plain steamed pudding, with 2—3 oz. dried fruit and 2 level teaspoons mixed spice added with the sugar.

CHOCOLATE PUDDING. Plain steamed pudding, with 3 level tablespoons cocoa added with the sugar and ½—1 oz. sugar, or syrup added with the liquid.

JAM OR MARMALADE PUDDING. Put 2 tablespoons of jam or marmalade in the bottom of the basin.

Suet Crust Pudding

8 oz. plain flour	1 oz. grated suet, or other
A pinch of salt	fat
2 level teaspoons baking powder	1 oz. grated raw potato
	Water to mix (about 4 tablespoons)

Mix together the flour, salt and baking powder. Add the suet (if other fat is used rub this into the flour, etc., until the mixture resembles breadcrumbs), grated potato and enough water to mix to a stiff consistency. Roll out ¾ of the mixture, line a greased 7in. basin with this. Fill the basin with fruit, and sugar (approximately 1½lb. fruit plus 2—3 oz. sugar) moisten the edge of the pastry with water. Roll out the remaining ¼ of pastry and cover the contents of the basin with this. Press the edges well together. Steam for 1—1½ hours.

Potter Pudding

2½ oz. margarine	6 oz. plain flour
3 oz. sugar	4 level teaspoons baking powder
2 dried eggs, dry	3 oz. breadcrumbs
4 tablespoons water	A little milk
Flavouring essence	2 oz. raisins, or ½ lb. apples, or 2 oz. jam or marmalade

Cream the margarine and sugar with the dried eggs, adding the water gradually during creaming. Add essence, sift the flour and baking powder and add to the creamed mixture. Add the breadcrumbs and sufficient milk to make a soft consistency. Grease a pudding basin and place the raisins or jam, or peeled and sliced apples in the bottom. Add the pudding mixture and cover with greased paper. Steam 1½ hours.

Jack Horner Pudding

6 oz. plain flour	Water to mix
2 level teaspoons baking powder	1 lb. fresh fruit or 6 oz. dried apricots or apple soaked overnight.
½ teaspoon salt	
1½ oz. suet or fat	Sugar to sweeten or saccharine
1½ oz. grated raw potato	

Mix flour, baking powder and salt. Rub in fat or add suet. Add potato. Mix to a stiff dough with water. Roll out ½ in. thick and the size of a saucepan top. Put fruit into pan with the sugar and a little water if fresh fruit is used or cover with water if dried fruit is used. When boiling put in the pastry round and cook about 30—45 minutes, dish up with fruit piled on pastry.

BAKED PUDDINGS

Apple Charlotte

1 lb. apples, or other fruit	½ level teaspoon cinnamon, nutmeg or mixed spice
6 oz. breadcrumbs	
2—3 oz. sugar	
	2 oz. margarine melted

Prepare the fruit, and cut it into thin slices. Mix together the breadcrumbs, sugar, spice and melted margarine. Arrange a layer of the breadcrumb mixture in a greased pint size pie dish, then a layer of fruit, and continue filling the pie dish with alternate layers of breadcrumbs and fruit until all the ingredients are used up finishing with a layer of the breadcrumb mixture. Bake in a moderate oven for ¾—1 hour. Serve hot.

VARIATIONS OF APPLE CHARLOTTE

PRUNE PUDDING. Replace apples by ¼ lb. prunes, soaked, stoned and cut into pieces.

CHOCOLATE APPLE CHARLOTTE. Add 2 level tablespoons cocoa to the breadcrumbs.

APPLE MARMALADE CHARLOTTE. Add 4—6 level tablespoons marmalade to the breadcrumb mixture to replace the sugar.

Cottage Pudding

8 oz. plain flour	3 oz. fat
Pinch salt	1 dried egg, dry
4 level teaspoons	3 oz. sugar
baking powder	Milk to mix (about $\frac{1}{4}$ pint)

Mix together the flour, salt and baking powder. Rub the fat
into this mixture. Add the dried egg, sugar and enough milk to
make the mixture to a soft consistency. Turn the mixture into a
greased Yorkshire pudding tin, and bake in a moderate oven from
30—40 minutes. Cut into squares and serve with custard or other
sauce.

VARIATIONS OF COTTAGE PUDDING

EVE'S PUDDING. 2 lb. apples or 1—2 lb. other fruit prepared
and put into a pie dish and covered with the cottage pudding
mixture.

COTTAGE FRUIT PUDDING. Cottage pudding,⎫ Add with
with 2—3 oz. dried fruit, 2 level teaspoons mixed spice.⎬ sugar.

GINGER COTTAGE PUDDING. Cottage pudding, with
3—4 level teaspoons ginger added with sugar.

(N.B.—Some of the sugar in the cottage pudding recipe may be
replaced by syrup in the Ginger Cottage Pudding.

MILK PUDDINGS

Semolina Pudding

4 level tablespoons	1 pint milk, fresh, house-
semolina	hold or tinned
1 level tablespoon	Grated nutmeg
sugar	Pinch of salt

Mix the semolina, sugar and salt with a little of the cold
liquid. Boil the remaining liquid and when boiling, pour it into
the blended semolina. Mix well, return to the pan, stir until it
boils and boil 5 minutes or cook 15 minutes over hot water.
Pour the mixture into a pie dish and grate a little nutmeg on top.
Bake in a moderate oven for about $\frac{1}{2}$ hour till brown on top.

American Bread Pudding

3—4 oz. bread cut in	1 tablespoon sugar
small cubes	1 egg reconstituted
(including crusts)	Pinch of salt
1 pint milk	1 teaspoon vanilla or
$\frac{1}{2}$ oz. margarine	$\frac{1}{4}$ teaspoon spice

Heat the milk and margarine and pour on the bread. Set
aside to cool. Add remaining ingredients, mix well and bake
until set in a moderate oven.

Variations. Spread top with jam or marmalade before
serving ; or add little dried fruit before baking ; or add 2 tablespoons cocoa and an extra tablespoon sugar.

COLD SWEETS

Cornflour Mould

1½ to 2 oz. cornflour, custard powder, or arrowroot	Pinch of salt
	1 pint milk
1½ oz. sugar	Flavouring

Mix the cornflour, sugar and salt to a smooth paste with a little milk. Boil the rest of the milk, and add this slowly to the blended cornflour. Return the mixture to the pan, add the flavouring, bring to the boil, and stirring well all the time, boil the mixture 5 minutes or longer. Pour the mixture into a wetted mould, and leave till cold, and set before turning out.

VARIATIONS OF CORNFLOUR MOULD

CHOCOLATE MOULD. Cornflour Mould recipe with the addition of 2 level tablespoons cocoa added with the cornflour, sugar, etc.

COFFEE MOULD. Cornflour Mould recipe using ½ pint milk and ½ pint strong black coffee to make up the pint of liquid.

N.B.—The Coffee Mould may be found too sweet by some. If this is the case the sugar could be cut down to 1 oz.

Mexican Cream

2 level tablespoons dried egg, dry	2—4 level tablespoons sugar
	Pinch of salt
2 level tablespoons flour	1 pint moderately strong coffee
2—4 level tablespoons cocoa	Vanilla essence

Mix the dry ingredients together and mix to a smooth paste with a little coffee. Boil the remaining coffee. Pour on to the other ingredients, return to the pan and boil 5 minutes. Add vanilla and pour into individual glasses or a serving dish. Serve cold.

Fruit Creams

½ lb. fruit	2 level dessertspoons semolina
½ pt. milk	
Colouring if necessary	Sugar to taste

Stew the fruit in as little water as possible. Boil the milk, sprinkle on the semolina. Stir until the mixture thickens. Allow to cook 15 minutes. Add the stewed fruit to the semolina, gradually, whisking all the time. Beat well 2—3 minutes. Add the sugar and suitable colouring. Serve cold.

YOUR VITAMIN A B C D

VITAMINS? WHAT IS THE GOOD OF THEM? WHAT DO THEY DO?

Well, Vitamins give you just that little something that makes all the difference between your just rubbing along—if that—and feeling absolutely fine, full of life and energy all the time. So it's worth while doing something about Vitamins, isn't it? Especially when it's as simple as A B C to learn all one needs to know of them.

These food substances are so important that the Government has taken certain especial steps in regard to them during war time.

For example, Vitamins A and D are added to our margarine; the national flour, from which our bread is made, is milled so as to contain far more Vitamin B than is contained in white flour, and the Government consistently encourages the greatest possible production and consumption of vegetables, which are our main source of Vitamin C, and a very rich source, too. Then there is the Government's special 'Vitamin Scheme' for children up to 5 years of age and for expectant mothers, on which further information is given in the last paragraph of this leaflet.

Well, to come back to the Vitamin A B C. It is on the next page. You will find it well worth while to read it carefully and to refresh your memory with it from time to time.

VITAMIN	WHAT IT DOES
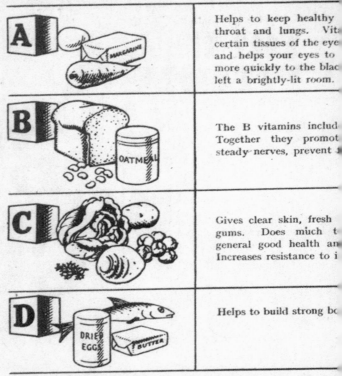 **A**	Helps to keep healthy throat and lungs. Vit. certain tissues of the eye and helps your eyes to more quickly to the blac. left a brightly-lit room.
B	The B vitamins includ. Together they promot. steady nerves, prevent s.
C	Gives clear skin, fresh gums. Does much t. general good health an. Increases resistance to i.
D	Helps to build strong bo.

Enemies of VITAMINS

AIR, WATER, HEAT. Too much of any of these will destroy the Vitamin C. Therefore, have your vegetables as fresh as possible. Best of all, grow them yourself. (The Ministry of Agriculture's free Cropping Plan which you can get from your bookstall or from the Ministry of Agriculture, Africa House, Kingsway, London, W.C.2, shows you how to get a regular supply of fresh vegetables all through the year from a small garden or plot).

Wash your vegetables in salted water but do not soak them overlong. Shred them before cooking so as to cook quickly. Cook in as little boiling salted water as possible, and keep the lid on the pan.

And remember, reheating or keeping vegetables hot for any length of time destroys their Vitamin C.

WHERE YOU GET IT

g of nose, also keeps n infection ccustomed r you have	Main sources : Your rations of butter and margarine. Also fish liver oil. Dried or fresh eggs. Carrots ; green vegetables. Milk. Cheese.
substances. digestion,	Main sources : National bread and flour. Dried or fresh eggs. Dried peas, beans and lentils. Oatmeal. Bacon. Milk. Cheese.
n, healthy stablishing at vitality.	Main sources : Parsley, brussels sprouts, spinach, cabbage, watercress, cauliflower, swedes, potatoes. Rose-hips, blackcurrants, orange juice.
ound teeth.	Main sources : Your rations of butter and margarine. Fish liver oil. Herrings and other oily fish. Dried or fresh eggs. Milk. Cheese.

How to get the VITAMIN C you need

Every day you need

2 or 3 tablespoonfuls of lightly cooked green vegetables; or swedes when green vegetables are unobtainable.

As well as

3 or 4 freshly cooked jacket potatoes

and a good helping of salad including shredded raw green vegetables, not forgetting Brussels sprouts, spinach and cabbage. Garnish liberally with parsley, mustard and cress and watercress, as these are very important sources of Vitamin C.

All these are required by **every person, every day.**

Ring the changes in the salad and green vegetables of course— not only according to season, but from day to day. And don't forget root vegetables—carrots, turnips, swedes. Swedes are a good source of Vitamin C. Remember too, how important it is for each person to have at least 1 lb. of potatoes a day.

HINTS AND RECIPES

An alphabet of vitamins in this one meal!

National bread and butter or margarine, some raw green salad, a piece of cheese and a glass of milk. The children should, of course, take some of their "priority" milk this way. For grown-ups, try cocoa or coffee made with household milk, or household milk flavoured with meat or vegetable extract.

School children having this for their mid-day meal every day grew stronger, healthier, and quicker than children having the usual meal of "meat and two veg." You'll find it a splendid lunch or dinner for grown-ups, too—the heaviest manual worker, the girl in shop or office, and the child of two and upwards, all are the better for this "Health Meal" three or four times a week. Better still, every day.

Gold and white salad

If you have one of those handy little potato peelers, use it to shave thin slivers of carrot and turnip; otherwise shave as thinly as possible with a sharp knife. Allow two or three small carrots and turnips per person. Do the same to some cheese; about an ounce per person. If the cheese is crumbly, grate it. Pile lightly in dish in pyramid form, on a good bed of shredded raw heart of cabbage or other greens, surround with a wreath of parsley or watercress.

Savoury Potato Salad

Cut cold potatoes in thick slices. Spread each slice thinly with meat or vegetable extract. Shred a small cabbage, mix it with a tablespoonful of chopped mint, arrange all on a dish, and sprinkle with chopped parsley.

Grow your own!

Even if you have no garden, you can have fresh-picked parsley or mustard and cress, for these both grow well in window-boxes or flower-pots. Or mustard and cress can be grown on damp flannel. Remember—the fresher the better for you—and the better the flavour!

Vitamins for Children up to five years old, and for expectant Mothers

Young children cannot eat enough greenstuff and other foods to give them all the vitamins their quickly-growing bodies and minds need. So the Government has made available **extra vitamins** in the form of fruit juice and cod liver oil for all children under 5 years of age; and for expectant mothers, too, because baby's needs begin before he is born. Don't think, because your little one seems "well enough" that he or she does not need these vitamin products. Only a plentiful supply of vitamins can ensure that children will grow and develop, and resist illness, as they should. Ask your local Food Office, Food Advice Centre, or Infant Welfare Clinic for particulars.

What's left in the
LARDER

SOME GENERAL TIPS

FOOD which has already been cooked only needs to be re-heated and is spoiled if cooked too much a second time. This is especially important to remember when using up left-over meat, fish and vegetables.

Dishes using cooked vegetables should, as far as possible, be served with a fresh salad, or a serving of freshly-cooked greens to make up for the Vitamin C lost in cooking and re-heating.

All dishes using left-overs need more seasoning than when uncooked food is used. This is because some of the natural flavour of the food is lost with re-heating.

Ways of

using up

left-overs

Using up
STALE BREAD

FAIRY TOAST

Cut wafer-thin slices of bread and bake in a moderate oven until crisp and golden brown. Store in airtight tin. This is a good standby to have in place of bread or plain biscuits and it will keep for months.

WHEATMEALIES

Half-dozen slices stale bread, $\frac{1}{4}$ in. thick

Cut into $\frac{1}{4}$-in. squares. Put on a baking sheet and bake in a slow oven till brown and crisp. Store in a tin. Serve with milk and sugar to taste.

SUMMER PUDDING

8 oz. fresh fruit (red or black if possible)   *$\frac{1}{2}$ pint water*
1–2 oz. sugar   *5 oz. stale bread, cut $\frac{1}{4}$–$\frac{1}{2}$ in. thick*

Stew the fruit with the sugar and water until tender. Cut a round of bread to fit the bottom of a basin (1 pint size) and line the side with fingers of bread cut slightly wider at one end than the other. Fit the fingers of bread together so that no basin shows through. Half fill the basin with stewed fruit. Cover with a layer of scraps of bread left from cutting the round, etc. Add the remaining fruit and cover with a layer of bread. Pour the rest of the juice over all and cover the pudding with a weighted plate or saucer. Leave for at least 2 hours to cool and set. Turn out carefully and serve with custard.

N.B.—Very juicy fruit does not require any water for stewing. Bottled fruit may be used if fresh fruit is not available.

SUMMER PUDDING

FISH CURRY

1 small onion, chopped	1 pint stock or water
1 small carrot, chopped	1 tablespoon vinegar
½–1 oz. dripping or cooking fat	1 tablespoon chutney
1 tablespoon curry powder	2 tablespoons sultanas
3 tablespoons flour	1–2 teaspoons salt
	12 oz. cooked flaked fish

Fry the onion and carrot in the dripping or fat. Stir in the curry powder and flour. Add the stock or water, stirring well. Bring to the boil and boil gently for 10-15 minutes. Add the vinegar, chutney, sultanas, salt and fish and heat until hot—about 5 minutes. Serve with mashed potatoes.

FISH PASTIES

8 oz. cooked fish	¼ pint white sauce
8 oz. mixed cooked vegetables	1 teaspoon salt
1 tablespoon vinegar	¼ teaspoon pepper
2 tablespoons chopped parsley	6 oz. shortcrust pastry

Mix together the fish, vegetables, vinegar, parsley, sauce and seasoning. Roll out the pastry thinly and cut into rounds about 6 in. in diameter. Place a portion of the filling on half of each round of pastry, damp the pastry edges, and fold over the remaining half of pastry. Seal the edges and bake in a moderate oven 25-30 minutes.

All Spoons Level

All Recipes for four

Using up
MEAT & VEGETABLES

RE-HEATING ROAST MEAT

Cut the meat in very thin slices and put it on a hot dish. Pour over boiling gravy or sauce to cover and serve at once. The hot gravy or sauce will heat the meat sufficiently and that "twice-cooked" flavour will be avoided.

BARLEY MINCE

3 oz. pearl barley	1 teaspoon beef extract
1½ pints water	1-2 teaspoons salt
1 teaspoon mixed herbs	½ teaspoon pepper
1 medium-sized onion, chopped	4 oz. cooked meat, minced or chopped
1 tablespoon flour	Gravy browning

Cook the barley in the water with the herbs and onion until tender, about 1 hour. Strain off the water and make up to ½ pint. Blend the flour with a little of this liquid, then add the remainder, stir until it thickens and boil for 5 minutes. Add the beef extract, seasoning, meat, barley and enough browning to give it a good colour. Warm through over a low heat for about 10 minutes. Serve very hot with vegetables.

DRESDEN PATTIES

1 oz. dripping	½-1 teaspoon salt
1 oz. plain flour	½ teaspoon pepper
¼ pint stock or vegetable water	1 teaspoon of a Worcester sauce
8 oz. cooked meat, chopped finely	4 rounds of bread, cut 1 in. thick (from 1 lb. loaf)
or 4 oz. cooked meat and 4 oz. chopped cooked vegetables	Chopped parsley

Heat the dripping, add the flour and cook until slightly browned. Gradually stir in the liquid, bring to the boil and cook for 5 minutes, stirring all the time. Add the meat, vegetables if used, seasoning and sauce. Keep hot while frying the bread. Trim the rounds of bread and cut a small circle from the centre of each. Fry rounds and circles in hot fat until golden brown. Drain well and fill the centres with the meat mixture. Place a small round of fried bread on top to form a lid and serve hot with chopped parsley sprinkled over.

DRESDEN PATTIE

METHOD ONE

Bake crusts in the oven until they are dry and crisp. Use a a rolling pin to crush them into fine crumbs. Store in an air-tight jar or tin. These crumbs are useful for coating food for frying, covering the tops of savoury dishes and for other dishes such as the Crumb Fudge given here.

METHOD TWO

Soak crusts in cold water and leave until soft. Squeeze very dry and return to the basin. Beat thoroughly to remove all lumps and make the mixture quite smooth. Soaked crusts are useful for making stuffing, bread puddings and steamed puddings.

CRUMB FUDGE

> 2 *tablespoons syrup*
> 2 *oz. margarine*
> 2 *oz. sugar*
> 2 *oz. cocoa*
> *Few drops vanilla, peppermint or orange essence*
> 4–6 *oz. dried crumbs*

Heat the syrup, margarine, sugar and cocoa gently until all is melted. Stir in the required flavouring and then the bread crumbs. Mix thoroughly and turn into a well-greased 7 in. sandwich tin ; spread evenly and mark lightly into fingers or squares. Leave for 24 hours and then use as a cake or sweet. This fudge improves with keeping for a day or two.

STUFFING WITH SOAKED SQUEEZED BREAD

6 oz. stale bread soaked and squeezed	3 tablespoons chopped parsley
1 onion or leek, or stick of celery, chopped finely	1–2 teaspoons mixed herbs
1 oz. suet or dripping or other fat	$\frac{1}{4}$ teaspoon pepper
	$\frac{1}{2}$–1 teaspoon salt

Mix together the bread and onion, add the suet or other fat grated or cut in small pieces. Add the remaining ingredients. Mix well.

CRUMB FUDGE

Using up
PUDDINGS

CRISPY PUDDING

Fry slices of cold steamed pudding in hot margarine until crisp on both sides ; drain well, sprinkle with sugar and serve very hot. Alternatively, the slices of pudding may be placed in a greased pie-dish sprinkled with sugar and dotted lightly with small knobs of margarine. Bake in hot oven 20 minutes.

FRUIT FOOL

Mix equal quantities of custard or milk pudding and stewed, fresh or dried fruit. Serve very cold with a sweet biscuit.

The Ministry of Food has compiled the " ABC of Cookery " which gives suggestions and methods for cooking and preparing food. Obtainable from H.M. Stationery Office or through any Bookseller. Price 1/- or 1/2 by post.

ISSUED BY THE MINISTRY OF FOOD 64111512
REVISED AND REPRINTED, DECEMBER, 1946

Herrings...

"Of all the fish that swim the sea" runs the old saying, "the herring is the King." Certainly whether it is a question of flavour, food value or cheapness, we have to agree that the herring is worthy of his crown.

Consider the herring's food value. It is a very cheap source of the best body-building protein. It is an oily fish and its oil is distributed throughout its flesh, not all contained in its liver as is the case with the cod and halibut. Herring oil not only supplies an extraordinary high number of calories or energy-giving units, but it also contains two vitamins, A & D. Vitamin A strengthens our resistance to disease and Vitamin D is essential for sound bones and teeth.

That is why the herring is such a valuable food for young and old. It is a tasty food, too. This leaflet gives you a number of ways of serving it, whether for breakfast, dinner, tea or supper.

MINISTRY OF FOOD · LEAFLET

No. 9

Devilled herrings

4 herrings, boned
2 dessertspoonsful mustard
 mixed with vinegar
1 tablespoon sugar
1 oz. margarine

¼ onion chopped finely
1 bay leaf
6 cloves
½ pint water

Mix the mustard, sugar and half the margarine to a paste. Spread on the herrings and roll up. Fry the onion, the bayleaf and the cloves in the remaining half ounce of margarine in a saucepan, add the rolled up herrings and ½ pint water, and simmer gently for 10 minutes. Baste herrings occasionally with the liquid. When cooked serve with sweet chutney.

Herring and tomato dish

4 herrings, boned
½ lb. tomatoes fresh or bottled
1 oz. cooking fat or dripping
4 cloves
1 bayleaf

3 tablespoons plain flour
¼ pint milk or vegetable stock
2 teaspoons made mustard
1 lb. cooked mashed potato

Cut the herrings into pieces. Place in a greased casserole with the tomatoes (skinned and sliced fresh). Melt the fat, fry the cloves and bayleaf in it for 2-3 minutes. Add the flour, and the liquid. Bring to the boil, and boil for 2-3 minutes. Add the mustard, season well, and pour over the contents in the dish. Cover with the potato and bake for ½ hour in a moderate oven

Baked herrings

4 herrings boned
2 small onions if liked
 (cut into slices)

A few peppercorns
Salt

Season the insides of the fillets with a little salt, and roll each piece round a piece of onion. Pack closely into a greased pie dish or casserole. Sprinkle the top with salt and a few peppercorns. Cover with a piece of greaseproof paper and bake in a moderate oven for about 10 minutes. Then remove the paper, and allow the fish to brown for a further 5 minutes.

Baked stuffed herrings

4 herrings, boned

Stuffing

2 oz. breadcrumbs or stale bread soaked and squeezed
¼ oz. melted dripping or other fat
2 tablespoons chopped parsley
1 strip of lemon rind if available
½ teaspoon thyme
1 dried egg reconstituted

Salt and pepper

Mix together the bread, parsley, chopped lemon rind, and thyme and season well. Add the fat. Bind with the egg. Season the insides of the fish with salt and pepper, spread with stuffing and fold back into shape. Lay them in a greased fireproof dish and bake as for "Baked Herrings."

Herring salad

4 boned, flaked cooked herring
1½ lb. sliced cooked potatoes
1 small onion or leek, finely chopped
2 tomatoes, sliced
6 prunes—soaked 24 hours and chopped
2 tablespoons raw grated turnip or swede
Salt and pepper
4 tablespoons salad dressing
½ lb. shredded raw cabbage heart
2 tablespoons chopped parsley

Mix all ingredients except cabbage and parsley with sufficient dressing to moisten well. Pile on a bed of shredded cabbage and sprinkle with chopped parsley.

Pickled herrings

1 pint of vinegar
1 pint of water
Salt to taste
20 peppercorns
5 bayleaves
2 level teaspoons allspice
4-5 onions sliced
4 slices lemon, if available
20 herrings (approx.)

Boil the vinegar with the water, salt, peppercorns, broken up bayleaves, allspice, and onions for half an hour. Add the slices of lemon and boil for five minutes longer. Simmer the fish in the liquid until it is soft. As they are done pack them in a stone jar with one or two thin slices of raw onion between each layer of fish. When the jar is full, cover with the hot liquid without straining it. Store in a cool place and the fish will jellify, and keep for several weeks.

Steamed herrings

(suitable for whole, or boned fish).

Place the fish to be steamed on a plate over a pan of boiling water. Put a knob or two of margarine or dripping on the fish. Cover with a pan lid or an inverted plate, and cook until the fish is tender, 10-15 minutes. Serve with one of the sauces given at the end of this leaflet.

Quick soused herrings

4 herrings, boned
1 dessertspoon pickling spice
1 bay leaf
Salt
A small amount of sliced onion, or spring onion
1-3rd pint water
1-3rd pint vinegar

Place the fish, either flat or rolled up in a frying pan or saucepan (preferably aluminium or enamel). Sprinkle with the spices, broken bay leaf, and onion, then cover with the vinegar, and water. Cover the frying pan with a lid, or an enamel plate to fit tightly. Heat slowly, and keep the pan just simmering for about 20 minutes to ½ an hour. Then remove from the liquor, and serve the fish hot, or leave the fish to cool in a covered pan if they are to be served cold with salad.

Herring roe savoury

8 soft roes
½ pint milk
1½ tablespoons plain flour

4 slices of toast
Salt and pepper
Chopped parsley

Rinse roes. Stew in the milk until they are tender, about 10-15 minutes. Place 2 roes on each piece of toast and keep hot. Mix the flour to a smooth paste with a little cold water, add the boiled milk. Return to the saucepan and stir until boiling. Boil 5 minutes, season well, and pour over the roes. Garnish with chopped parsley.

Mock oyster pudding

5 medium soft roes
2 oz. dried breadcrumbs
½ pint milk
1 oz. melted margarine

2 dried eggs reconstituted
1 teaspoon sugar
Salt and pepper
A little nutmeg

Rinse the roes, and drain well. Chop finely. Mix with the breadcrumbs, milk, margarine, eggs, sugar, seasoning and nutmeg. Turn into a greased piedish. Bake till golden brown in a moderately hot oven about 30 minutes.

Soused herrings

8 herrings, boned
1 onion
1 tablespoon mixed pickling spice

¼ pint vinegar
¼ pint water
1 teaspoon salt

Roll up the fish with a slice of onion inside each fish. Pack in a baking dish. Scatter pickling spice between the rolls, and add the remainder of the onion sliced. Sprinkle in salt, pour in vinegar and water mixed together, and bake in a slow oven for 1½ hours.

Herring pie

½ lb. grated raw potato
½ lb. grated raw apple
1 onion chopped
¼ teaspoon nutmeg

Salt and pepper
4 herrings, boned
1 teaspoon lemon substitute
6 oz. pastry

Grease a shallow dish and arrange half the potato, apple and onion on it. Sprinkle on the nutmeg seasoning and lemon substitute. Lay the herrings on top. Cover with the remainder of the potato, apple and onion mixture. Roll out the pastry. Cover the dish with it, and bake in a hot oven for 30 minutes.

Herring hot pot

1½ lb. potatoes peeled and sliced ¼ inch thick
4 herrings, boned
1 leek chopped

Salt and water
½ pint water

Place some potatoes in the bottom of a greased casserole then spread a herring over these, and sprinkle with some leek, and salt and pepper. Repeat this, and finish with a layer of potato. Pour over the water, and cook for

78

Fresh herrings

should be bright and silvery in appearance, the eyes clear and bright, not bloodshot or sunken.

To clean

Cut the head off the fish. Remove the insides, retaining the roes. To scale use the back of a knife and holding the fish by the tail, scrape firmly from the tail towards the head. Cut off the tail. Rinse the fish well in cold water.

To bone

Proceed as above, then with a sharp knife, or kitchen scissors split down the belly of the fish from the head end to the tail. Open the fish gently. Carefully loosen the small bones on each side of the back bone with the scissors. Starting at the head end prise up the backbone with the thumb and forefinger and pull it steadily away from the flesh. Rinse the fish well and place on a board. Stand the board on a slant to drain the fish.

Grilled herrings

(suitable for whole or boned fish).

If the fish is to be grilled whole cut the flesh in three or four places across the back. Season the fish well. Put a knob or two of margarine or dripping on the fish. Place under a hot grill and grill till brown on both sides. Serve with a suitable sauce.

Fried herrings

(suitable for whole or boned fish).

1. Without fat

This method is only possible with a very thick frying pan. Sprinkle the pan with salt, heat the pan, shaking it occasionally until very hot. Place the herrings in the pan, and fry on both sides till brown, and crisp. Serve hot.

2. Fried in shallow fat

Bone and wipe the fish, and dip in flour, or oatmeal mixed with salt, and pepper. Heat some fat in a frying pan until a faint blue haze rises, put in the fish, and cook until brown, turning on both sides.

Hard roes

These may be washed, dipped in flour or egg and breadcrumbs and fried in a little hot fat till golden brown.

They may also be boiled gently till tender, about 15 minutes, allowed to become cold and served with salad.

Sauces to serve with herrings

Foundation melted butter sauce

1 oz. margarine   ½ pint hot water
2 tablespoons plain flour

Melt the margarine and mix in the flour. Cook for 2-3 minutes. Pour in the hot water, bring gradually to the boil, and boil very gently for 2-3 minutes. Add seasoning and capers, fennel or mustard. See below.

Caper Sauce

Add 1 tablespoon capers, or pickled nasturtium seeds cut in two, or coarsely chopped, and 1 dessertspoon vinegar from the capers to ½ pint foundation sauce.

Fennel Sauce

Add 2 tablespoons chopped fennel to ½ pint foundation sauce.

Mustard Sauce

Mix together 2 teaspoons mustard and 2 teaspoons vinegar, and stir into ½ pint foundation sauce.

How to preserve
TOMATOES

When tomatoes are available the wise housewife will preserve some for use in the winter. They are valuable then, not only for the colour and flavour they give to dishes, but also for the protective vitamins they contain. Don't forget that you get more food value from bottled tomatoes if they are eaten "straight from the jar," since further cooking destroys some of their vitamins.

CHOOSING PRESERVING JARS
AND RUBBER RINGS

There are many different kinds of preserving jars, but they all work in the same way. The jar, filled with the hot sterilised tomatoes, is closed with a glass or metal lid resting on a rubber ring to make the join airtight. While the contents of the jar are cooling the lid is held tightly in place by a screwband, metal clip, weight, second metal lid or other mechanical grip. When the jar is cold, the lid is held firmly in place by the vacuum formed in the jar. Once the jar is sealed in this way it no longer depends on the tightness of the screwband, clip, or other grip to keep it airtight.

Before buying jars, make sure there are no chips, ridges, etc., on the mouth, which might prevent the lid and rubber ring from fitting properly. If you use the special lids sold to fit on jam jars, choose jars that have smooth and quite circular mouths, and make certain that the lids fit properly. Test before using (see below).

When buying rubber rings, take a sample jar or ring with you to get the right size. Good rings feel elastic and will spring back after slight stretching.

TESTING JARS BEFORE USE

Fill the jar with water, put on the rubber ring, lid and screwband, clip, or other grip. Wipe the outside of the jar and stand upside down for half an hour; if the water leaks out, examine the jar for defects. If a jar leaks when first tested, a different rubber ring or two rings may help. With the clip type it may be necessary to bend the clip slightly to make it grip more tightly; or a penny pushed under the centre of the clip may help. It is essential to test all jam jars in this way before using them for bottling.

STORAGE

Bottled tomatoes should be stored in a cool dark place; light destroys the colour of tomatoes and their vitamin C. A label with the date of bottling will show which jar should be used first. The screwbands, clips or other grips, should be removed and greased, and either put away in a dry place until next year, to prevent rusting, or, in the case of screwbands, they can be replaced on the jars, but should not be screwed down tightly.

SPECIAL NOTE.
The methods described in this leaflet are not suitable for bottling vegetables. A pressure cooker must be used.

method 1

PRESERVING TOMATOES
BY THE OVEN METHOD

Wash and drain the jars. There is no need to dry them.

Wash the tomatoes and pack them whole into the jars, filling almost to the top.

Put the jars in a very moderate oven (about 240° F.), covering with a tin to prevent discolouring. The jars must be placed on an asbestos mat, piece of cardboard or wood or several thicknesses of newspaper so that they do not touch the oven shelf.

Heat the jars until the tomatoes are thoroughly cooked and have shrunk a little. This takes at least $1\frac{1}{2}$ hours. It is most important that the tomatoes should be thoroughly cooked.

Prepare some boiling brine with $\frac{1}{2}$ oz. salt to 2 pints water. $\frac{1}{4}$ oz. sugar may be added to improve the flavour.

Put the rubber rings and lids in a pan of cold water, bring to the boil and keep boiling for 15 minutes to sterilize them. They must be hot when placed on the jars. With metal lids, fit the rubber rings on them before sterilizing if possible as they are difficult to handle when hot. Screwbands and clips need not be sterilized.

Remove the jars one at a time from the oven and fill to overflowing with the boiling brine. If the tomatoes have shrunk very much, before adding the boiling brine, quickly fill up with tomatoes from an extra bottle heated with the others. Put the hot rubber ring and lid on at once and fasten down with screwband, clip or other grip. Each jar must be sealed before the next jar is taken out of the oven. As the sealed jars cool, the screwbands may need tightening.

TESTING THE SEAL

After 24 hours, remove the screwband, clip or other grip, and lift each jar by its lid. If the lid comes off, the seal is imperfect and the tomatoes should be eaten within a few days or resterilized by heating again just as described above. If the jars can be lifted by the lid the seal is perfect.

N.B.

Some types of closure do not have a removable grip and the seal cannot be tested.

Remember that even a perfect seal is no guarantee that the tomatoes will keep, unless the sterilizing has been done properly. The instructions must be followed carefully.

method 2

PRESERVING TOMATOES IN
THEIR OWN JUICE USING A DEEP PAN

This method needs a deep pan of some kind as described in "Preserving Tomatoes in Brine."

Wash and drain the jars and lids; put the rubber rings to soak in cold water.

Skin the tomatoes by placing them in boiling water for half a minute and then at once into cold water. After this the skins can be slipped off easily. Cut medium or large tomatoes into halves or quarters.

Pack the tomatoes tightly into the jars, sprinkling salt on each layer (¼ oz. salt to 2 lb. tomatoes). A teaspoon of sugar to 2 lb. of tomatoes improves the flavour. Press the tomatoes well down in the jar but add no liquid. It is sometimes useful to stew a few tomatoes in a pan, so that they can be used to complete the filling of the jars.

The lids and rubber rings should then be put in position and the rest of the method carried out just as in "Preserving Tomatoes in Brine," (method 3).

After 24 hours test the seals as already described in the "Oven Method."

method 3

PRESERVING TOMATOES
IN BRINE USING A DEEP PAN

For this method you need a pan deep enough to allow the jars to be completely covered with water. A sterilizer, zinc bath, large fish kettle, or even a bucket will do. It must be arranged so that the jars do not touch the bottom or sides of the pan. A false bottom can be made by nailing together strips of wood in trellis fashion, or a layer of straw, folded newspaper or cloth can be used. If no lid is available, use a pastry board.

Wash and drain the jars and lids; put the rubber rings to soak in cold water.

Make a brine by dissolving ½ oz. salt in 2 pints water; ¼ oz. of sugar may be added to improve the flavour.

Wash the tomatoes thoroughly and pack them tightly into the jars almost to the top. Fill the jars to overflowing with the COLD brine.

Put the rubber rings and lids in position and fasten with the screwbands, clips or other grip. Screwbands should be tightened up and THEN UNSCREWED HALF A TURN TO ALLOW FOR EXPANSION.

Stand the jars on the false bottom in the pan so that they don't touch one another or the sides of the pan. Cover the jars completely with cold water. Put on the lid. Heat slowly to 195° F. (this should take not less than 1½ hours). Keep at this temperature for half an hour. If a thermometer is not available, heat up to simmering point in 1½ hours and then simmer for half an hour.

Take out some hot water with a cup or jug. Holding them by the shoulder, lift one jar at a time out of the pan, stand it on a wooden table or board and tighten the screwband or see that the clip or other grip is holding properly. Put the jar aside to cool. With the screwband type don't take out several jars at once. Each jar must be screwed up with the least possible delay while it is still hot. As the jars cool, the screwbands may need tightening up further.

After 24 hours test the seals as already described in the "Oven Method."

method 4

PULPING TOMATOES

This method needs a deep pan as described in "Preserving Tomatoes in Brine."

Wash and drain the jars and lids. Put the rubber rings to soak in cold water. Put the jars somewhere to get hot.

Skin (see previous method) and cut up tomatoes and cook in a covered saucepan with ¼ teaspoon salt to every 2 lb. tomatoes, adding just enough water to prevent burning. Very little water is needed. When the tomatoes are thoroughly pulped pour at once into the hot jars. Wipe the top of the jar with a clean cloth and seal immediately with rubber ring, lid and screwband, clip or other grip. Tighten the screwband up and THEN UNSCREW HALF A TURN TO ALLOW FOR EXPANSION.

Put the jars in BOILING water in a deep pan as described in "Preserving Tomatoes in Brine," bring to the boil and boil for 10 minutes. The jars must be completely covered by the water.

Remove the jars one at a time and tighten the screwband or see that the clip or other grip is properly in position. After cooling 24 hours test as described in the "Oven Method."

N.B.

Three of these methods are demonstrated in the film "Deep Pan Bottling," obtainable from the Central Film Library, London, S.W.7.

The Ministry of Food has compiled the A B C of Cookery, which is a comprehensive guide to cookery methods. Obtainable from H.M. Stationery Office, price 1s. 0d. or by post 1s. 2d.

Revised and Reprinted February 1947   Issued by the Ministry of Food   74114902.   S1-2800

CAKES
BISCUITS
and SCONES
without eggs

PLAIN CAKE FOUNDATION RECIPE

½ lb. plain flour and
4 teaspoons baking powder or
½ lb. self raising flour
Pinch of salt

3 oz. margarine
3 oz. sugar
1 teaspoon vanilla essence
Approx. ¼ pint milk and water

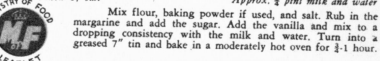

Mix flour, baking powder if used, and salt. Rub in the margarine and add the sugar. Add the vanilla and mix to a dropping consistency with the milk and water. Turn into a greased 7" tin and bake in a moderately hot oven for ¾-1 hour.

MINISTRY OF FOOD
MF
LEAFLET
No. 30

VARIATION

ROCK BUNS VARIATIONS

1 Foundation recipe with the addition of 4 oz. dried fruit and ½ teaspoon mixed spice, added with the sugar. Use as little liquid as possible for mixing so that the mixture is very stiff and will stand up in small heaps on a greased baking sheet. Bake in a hot oven for 10-15 minutes.

PLAIN FRUIT CAKE

2 As for rock buns, but make the mixture to a dropping consistency and turn into a greased 7" tin and bake in a moderate oven for ¾-1 hour.

GINGER CAKE

3 Use the foundation recipe and add 2 teaspoons ground ginger and ½ teaspoon mixed spice with the flour. Put in a 7" tin and bake in moderate oven for ¾-1 hour.

CHOCOLATE CAKE

4 Use the foundation recipe and add 3 tablespoons cocoa with the sugar. Put in a 7" tin and bake in moderate oven for ¾-1 hour.

RASPBERRY BUNS

5 Foundation recipe, but 2 oz. instead of 3 oz. sugar and 1 tablespoon jam, raspberry if possible. Save 1 dessertspoon sugar for coating and use only enough milk to mix to a stiff dough which can be cut into 12 equal pieces. Form into buns and make a hole in the middle. Put in a little jam and pull the dough over to cover it. Roll in sugar and place on a greased baking sheet. Bake in a hot oven for 10 minutes.

FRUIT CAKE

2 oz. margarine or cooking fat	1 oz. sugar
½ lb. plain flour and	4 oz. chopped dates or other
4 teaspoons baking powder or	dried fruit
¼ lb. self-raising flour	⅜ pint milk and water
Pinch of salt	3 saccharin tablets

Rub the fat into the flour, baking powder if used and salt. Add the sugar and dried fruit. Mix to a soft consistency with milk and water in which the saccharin tablets have been dissolved. Turn the mixture into a greased 6" tin and bake in a moderate oven for about 1 hour.

BUN LOAF

2 oz. margarine or lard
½ lb. plain flour
Pinch of salt
2 oz. sugar
½ teaspoon mixed spice
3 oz. chopped dried fruit
¼ pint milk and water

1 tablespoon vinegar
1 teaspoon bicarbonate of soda

Rub the margarine or lard into the flour and salt. Add the sugar, spice and dried fruit and mix well. Add the milk and water and vinegar and beat well. Lastly, mix in the soda dissolved in a little warm water and turn the mixture into a greased 6" tin. Bake in a moderate oven for ¾ hour.

GINGERBREAD CAKE

½ lb. self-raising flour
6 oz. syrup
1 teaspoon ground ginger

1 teaspoon bicarbonate of soda
¼ pint tepid water

Place the flour and syrup in a basin. Mix the ginger and soda with the tepid water, add to the flour and syrup and mix all together. Turn into a greased tin, about 11" x 7", and bake in a moderate oven for about 1¼ hours. Do not cut for 2 days.

QUEEN CAKES

2½ oz. margarine
2 oz. sugar
1 tablespoon syrup
Few drops vanilla essence
6 oz. self-raising flour or

6 oz. plain flour and
3 teaspoons baking powder
Pinch of salt
¼ pint milk and water
1½ oz. currants

Cream the margarine and sugar together until light, then add the syrup and essence and beat well again. Sieve the flour, baking powder if used, and salt and add to the creamed mixture with the milk and water. Add the currants, mix well and put into greased bun tins. Bake in a moderate oven for 20-25 minutes. This quantity makes approximately 1 dozen cakes.

CHOCOLATE CAKE

3 oz. margarine or fat
7 oz. plain flour
1 teaspoon baking powder
½ teaspoon salt
1½ oz. cocoa
3 oz. sugar
¼ pint warm milk and water
1 teaspoon bicarbonate of soda

1 tablespoon vinegar
½ teaspoon vanilla essence

Rub the margarine or fat into the flour, baking powder and salt. Add the cocoa and sugar and mix with the milk and water. Dissolve the soda in the vinegar and add to the cake mixture with the essence. Mix, turn into a greased 6" tin and bake in a moderate oven for 1½ hours.

CHOCOLATE SPONGE

½ lb. self-raising flour
¼ teaspoon salt
2 tablespoons cocoa
3 oz. sugar
1 tablespoon syrup

12-14 tablespoons hot water
1 teaspoon bicarbonate of soda
3 oz. margarine or lard
Vanilla essence

Mix the flour, salt, cocoa and sugar together. Dissolve the syrup in the water and add the bicarbonate of soda. Melt the margarine or lard and mix all the ingredients together including the essence, but do not beat the mixture, which should be very soft. Divide the mixture evenly into two 8" sandwich tins and bake in a moderately hot oven for 20 minutes. When cool use jam or a chocolate or cream filling between the two layers.

DRIPPING CAKE

½ lb. self-raising flour or
½ lb. plain flour and
4 teaspoons baking powder
½ teaspoon salt
½ teaspoon mixed spice
2 oz. clarified dripping

3 oz. sugar
3 oz. currants
or sultanas
¼ pint milk

Sift the flour, baking powder, if used, salt and spice together. Rub in the dripping and add the sugar and fruit. Mix to a soft consistency with the milk and turn into a greased 6" cake tin. Bake in a moderate oven for 50 minutes.

N.B.—If hard mutton dripping is used, it may be slightly warmed to make it easier to rub in.

DIGESTIVE BISCUITS

2 oz. fat
6 oz. self-raising flour or
6 oz. plain flour and
3 teaspoons baking powder

3 oz. oatmeal
1 oz. sugar
Pinch of salt
About ¼ pint water

Rub the fat into the dry ingredients. Add just enough water to bind the dough. Knead a little and roll out to less than ¼" thick. Cut into rounds. Place on a floured baking sheet and bake in a fairly cool oven until the biscuits are coloured. Makes 20-24 biscuits with a 3" cutter.

ANZAC BISCUITS

3 oz. margarine
3 oz. sugar
1 tablespoon syrup
½ teaspoon vanilla essence

1 teaspoon bicarbonate of soda
2 tablespoons hot water
3 oz. plain flour
½ lb. rolled oats

Cream margarine and sugar. Add syrup and vanilla essence. Dissolve bicarbonate of soda in hot water and add. Add flour and then oats to give a stiff consistency. Place teaspoons of the mixture on a tray 2 inches apart and cook in a moderate oven for 20 minutes. Makes 36 biscuits.

ALL SPOONS LEVEL

GINGER BISCUITS

2 oz. sugar
2 oz. syrup
2 oz. margarine or cooking fat
½ lb. plain flour
½ teaspoon mixed spice

2 teaspoons ginger
Lemon substitute
1 teaspoon bicarbonate soda
1 tablespoon tepid water

Melt in a pan the syrup, sugar and margarine or fat. Pour into a bowl. Add some flour and the spice, ginger and lemon substitute. Stir well. Dissolve the bicarbonate of soda in a tablespoon of tepid water, and add to mixture. Continue stirring, gradually adding more flour. Finish the process by turning out the mixture on to a well-floured board. Knead in the remainder of the flour. Roll out and cut into shapes. Cook in a moderate oven for 15-20 minutes. Makes approximately 24 biscuits.

SHORTBREAD

2 oz. margarine
3 oz. flour

1 oz. sugar

Rub the margarine into the flour and sugar. Knead into a dough without adding any water. Roll out to about ⅜" and cut into biscuits. Bake in a cool oven until pale brown.

CHOCOLATE FILLING

½ oz. margarine
2 oz. cocoa
2 oz. sugar

2 tablespoons strong black
coffee or
2 tablespoons water and
1 teaspoon vanilla essence

Melt the margarine. Remove from the heat and add the cocoa and sugar. Beat in the coffee, or water and essence, until mixture becomes a good spreading consistency.

CREAM FILLINGS

1
1 oz. margarine
1 oz. sugar
4 tablespoons household milk,
dry

1 tablespoon warm water
Flavouring to taste

Cream margarine and sugar till white and smooth. Add the milk and water gradually, beating well in till quite smooth. Add a few drops of flavouring to taste.

2
1 tablespoon custard
powder or cornflour
¼ pint milk

1 oz. margarine
½ oz. sugar
Flavouring

Blend the custard powder or cornflour with a little cold milk. Warm the rest of the milk in a saucepan. Add it to the custard powder and return to the pan. Stir over heat till well cooked. Put aside to cool. Cream margarine and sugar together very well; beat in the thick custard, add flavouring, and continue to beat till creamy. This makes about ¼ pint of cream similar in texture to whipped cream.

PLAIN SCONES

½ lb. self-raising flour or
½ lb. plain flour and
4 teaspoons baking powder

1 teaspoon salt
1 oz. margarine
A bare ¼ pint milk

Mix the flour, baking powder (if used) and salt together, rub in the margarine. Mix to a soft dough with milk. Turn on to a floured board and roll out to ¾" in thickness. Cut into 8 rounds or triangles; put on a greased baking sheet and bake in a hot oven for 15 minutes. Serve hot or cold with a savoury or sweet sandwich filling.

SWEET SCONES

Plain scone recipe with 1 oz. sugar added after fat has been rubbed in. Proceed as before.

FRUIT SCONES

Plain scone recipe with the addition of 1 oz. sugar and 1 oz. dried fruit added after the fat has been rubbed in. Proceed as before.

GIRDLE SCONES

½ lb. plain flour and
4 teaspoons baking powder or
½ lb. self-raising flour
½ teaspoon salt

½-1 oz. lard or cooking fat
Milk and water to mix
(approx. ¼ pint)

Mix the flour, baking powder if used, and salt. Rub in the fat and add enough milk and water to mix to a soft dough. Turn on to a floured board, knead lightly and roll out quickly to ¼" thick. Cut into triangles and place on a fairly hot girdle. Bake steadily until well risen and a light brown colour underneath; turn, and bake on the second side until cooked in the centre (the time required for cooking is from 10-15 minutes). This quantity makes about 14 scones 3" x 2".

N.B.—An electric hot plate or thick frying pan may be used in place of a girdle.

For hints on mixing and baking cakes see "The A.B.C. of Cookery" published by H.M. Stationery Office, price 1/-.

Making the most of the SUGAR

THE best way of stretching the sugar ration is by making full use of other sweetenings such as saccharin, honey, syrup or treacle, jam, marmalade, sweetened condensed milk and dried fruit.

MINISTRY OF FOOD
LEAFLET No. 21

USING Honey Syrup Treacle

Melt syrup, treacle or honey slightly before using. This makes it easier to measure and prevents using too much. Any tins or jars which have been emptied should be rinsed out with a little hot water. This sweetened water can be used when mixing puddings, making sauces or stewing fruit.

HONEY & SYRUP IN JAM, MARMALADE OR BOTTLED FRUIT

Honey and syrup can be used to replace up to half the sugar used in jam and marmalade. For example, if the recipe needs 3 lb. sugar you could use instead 1½ lb. sugar and 1½ lb. honey or syrup. Make sure the fruit is thoroughly cooked before the sugar and honey or syrup are added. This is important as if long boiling takes place afterwards sugar crystals may separate out.

Honey or syrup may be used in bottling fruit but the flavour will be noticeable. Use the same amount of honey or syrup as you would sugar.

HONEY & SYRUP IN STEWED FRUIT

Use in the same way as sugar adding either before or after cooking.

CHOCOLATE SPONGE

8 oz. self-raising flour
¼ teaspoon salt
2 tablespoons cocoa
3 oz. sugar
1 tablespoon syrup
12-14 tablespoons hot water
1 teaspoon bicarbonate soda
3 oz. margarine or lard
Vanilla essence

Mix the flour, salt, cocoa and sugar together. Dissolve the syrup in the water and add the bicarbonate of soda. Melt the fat and mix all the ingredients together, including the essence, but do not beat the mixture, which should be very soft. Divide the mixture evenly into two 8 inch sandwich tins and bake in a moderately hot oven for 20 minutes. When cool use jam or a sweet spread as a filling between the two layers.

HONEY BISCUITS

2½ oz. margarine
1 oz. sugar
2 tablespoons honey
6 oz. self-raising flour or
6 oz. plain flour and 3 teaspoons baking powder
1 teaspoon cinnamon
Pinch of salt

Cream the margarine and sugar. Add the honey, work in the flour, cinnamon and salt. Roll out until ¼ inch thick. Cut into rounds, place on a baking sheet, and bake in a moderately hot oven for 10 minutes. This quantity makes approximately 40-50 biscuits.

ALL SPOONS ARE Level

PEPPERMINT STICKS

1 lb. syrup
5 tablespoons water
Pinch cream of tartar or
1 teaspoon vinegar

½ teaspoon peppermint essence
or
A few drops of oil of peppermint

Bring the syrup and water to the boil slowly, and add the cream of tartar or vinegar. Boil until a little snaps when tested in cold water. Add the peppermint, and pour on to a greased plate. Leave till the edge takes the mark of the finger. Fold the sides of the mixture into the centre. Remove from the plate and pull the mixture until it becomes lighter in colour. Cut into 12 or 18 pieces, and pull into sticks. Leave to set on a flat greased surface.

CHOCOLATE CRUNCH

1 oz. margarine
4 tablespoons syrup
1 tablespoon cocoa

Pinch of salt
4 oz. rolled oats or
barley flakes

Warm margarine and syrup and beat well. Add the cocoa and salt and beat again. Gradually work in the oats. Spread on a shallow greased tin (about 4 inch by 6 inch) and bake in a moderate oven for 20 minutes. Mark into fingers and cut when cold.

GINGERBREAD CAKE

8 oz. self-raising flour
6 oz. syrup
1 teaspoon ground ginger

1 teaspoon bicarbonate of soda
¼ pint tepid water

Place the flour and syrup in a basin. Mix the ginger and soda with the tepid water, add to the flour and syrup and mix all together. Turn into a greased tin, about 11 in. x 7 in., and bake in a moderate oven for about 1¼ hours. Do not cut for 2 days.

USING

Rinse empty jam jars with a little hot water and use this in sauces or for mixing puddings and cakes.

JAM BISCUITS

3 oz. fat
8 oz. flour

2 tablespoons milk
3 tablespoons jam

Rub fat into the flour till the consistency of breadcrumbs. Mix together the milk and the jam. Add this to the fat and flour, knead well. Roll out very thinly, cut in shapes and bake in a moderate oven for 15 minutes.

JAM SAUCE

1 tablespoon jam
¼ pint water

1 teaspoon cornflour or
custard powder or
2 teaspoons flour

Put the jam and water in a small pan and bring to the boil. Blend the cornflour, custard powder or flour with a little cold water (about 2 teaspoons), pour the boiling liquid on to this. Return to the pan and boil gently for 5 minutes, stirring carefully. Serve with steamed puddings.

EQUALITY PUDDING

2 oz. cooking fat or margarine
8 oz. plain flour
1½-2 tablespoons sugar
2 tablespoons jam

1 teaspoon bicarbonate
of soda
Approx. ¼ pint milk and
water

Rub the cooking fat or margarine into the flour and mix in the sugar. Add the jam, dissolve the soda in a little milk and mix the pudding to a soft dropping consistency. Turn into a greased basin, 1½ pint size, and steam for 2 hours. Serve with custard or a sweet sauce.

BREAD & MARMALADE PUDDING

4 oz. breadcrumbs
3-4 tablespoons marmalade

1 pint milk, fresh or household

Place half the breadcrumbs in a 1½ pint pie dish. Spread over the marmalade and cover with the remaining crumbs, adding the milk last. Bake in a moderately hot oven for 1-1½ hours, when the pudding should be set and golden brown.

SWISS ROLY POLY

6 oz. prepared rhubarb, or any
fresh fruit, chopped
2 tablespoons mixed dried
fruit

Pinch of mixed spice
2 tablespoons breadcrumbs
1 tablespoon any red jam
6 oz. pastry

Mix together the rhubarb, dried fruit, spice, breadcrumbs and jam for the filling. Roll the pastry to an oblong, spread with the filling and damp the edges. Roll up like a Swiss roll and seal the ends. Place on a greased tin, brush with milk and bake in a moderate oven for 30-40 minutes.

Dried Fruit

Dried fruit can be used to add sweetness to biscuits, cakes, puddings, pies and sandwich fillings. Stewed with fresh fruit it helps to save sugar as well as giving an interesting flavour.

FIG BISCUITS

PASTRY

8 oz. plain flour
Pinch of salt
2 oz. cooking fat
Water to mix

FILLING

2-3 oz. figs
4 tablespoons water
½ teaspoon ginger and
mixed spice
Few drops lemon essence

Mix the flour and salt and rub in the fat. Mix in water and work to a stiff dough. Chop up the figs and simmer in the water till quite soft. Add the spice, and lemon essence, and allow to become quite cold. Roll pastry out into an oblong 12 inch by 24 inch and ¼ inch thick. Spread half of the pastry with the filling, cover with the other half, bake in a hot oven for 10 minutes and cut into squares when cold. This quantity makes approximately 40 biscuits.

DATE FILLING

4 oz. dates
4 tablespoons water
2 teaspoons custard powder

1 teaspoon lemon essence
6 oz. short pastry

Stone the dates and stew in the water until soft. Mix the custard powder to a smooth paste with a little cold water. Add it to the dates with the lemon essence. Bring to the boil and cook for 2–3 minutes stirring the whole time. Press the dates on the side of the pan to help to break them down. Line a 7 inch tin with the pastry and spread over the filling. Bake in a hot oven for 20–30 minutes.

DRIED FRUIT FRITTERS

4 oz. plain flour and
2 teaspoons baking powder or
4 oz. self-raising flour
Pinch of salt

¼ pint water
2 oz. any dried fruit, chopped
Fat for frying

Mix the flour, baking powder if used, and salt to a batter with the water ; add the fruit. Fry in tablespoonfuls in hot fat until brown on both sides. Serve with a little sugar sprinkled over or with some melted syrup.

DATE FINGERS

2 oz. margarine
2 oz. syrup
3 oz. chopped dates
½ teaspoon almond essence

4 oz. barley kernels or flakes or rolled oats
2 oz. self-raising flour or
2 oz. plain flour and 1 teaspoon baking powder

Melt the margarine and syrup over gentle heat. Stir in the dates and almond essence. Mix the barley kernels or flakes or rolled oats with the flour and baking powder, if used, and stir into the ingredients in the pan. Spread out on a greased tin, pressing with damp fingers until the mixture is pressed down smoothly and about ½ inch in thickness. Bake in a moderate oven for 20–25 minutes. Leave for a few minutes to set and, while still warm, cut into fingers. Remove from the tin when cold.

BICARBONATE OF SODA IN STEWED FRUIT

A little bicarbonate of soda added to fruit while stewing will neutralise some of the acid, and the fruit will then need less sugar. Use ½ teaspoon of bicarbonate of soda to 1 lb. of fruit, and stir it in slowly at the end of the cooking.

N.B.—This is not suitable to use for jam making.

USING Saccharin

For sweetening, 3 to 4 standard tablets of saccharin are equal to 1 oz. of sugar.

FORTIFIED SUGAR

Saccharin tablets may be mixed with sugar. Crush 30 tablets, using a rolling pin, and mix with 8 oz. sugar. This mixture will then equal 1 lb. of sugar in sweetness. It may be stored in a covered jar and used as required. When using this "fortified" sugar only half the usual amount of sugar will be needed. For example, if a recipe normally requires 2 oz. sugar only 1 oz. of the fortified sugar will be required to give the same sweetening and if you generally have 1 teaspoon of sugar in tea or coffee only $\frac{1}{2}$ a teaspoon of fortified sugar will be needed.

SACCHARIN IN JAM & BOTTLED FRUIT

Saccharin should not be used in making jam as jam will not keep unless it contains the full amount of sugar.
Saccharin or fortified sugar may be used for bottling fruit. It should be dissolved in water in the same way as when making a sugar syrup for bottling.

SWEETENING CUSTARD, SAUCES & STEWED FRUIT

When saccharin only is used crush the tablets and stir in when cooking is finished. Better results are obtained by using the fortified sugar which may be added during cooking in the usual way.

PLAIN CAKE

3 oz. margarine	2 oz. sugar and
8 oz. plain flour and	7$\frac{1}{2}$ saccharin tablets (crushed)
4 teaspoons baking powder or	Milk to mix (about $\frac{1}{4}$ pint)
8 oz. self-raising flour	Flavouring to taste

Rub the margarine into the flour, add the baking powder (if used), and sugar. Dissolve the saccharin tablets in a little warm milk and add to the mixture with more milk to form a soft consistency. Turn into a greased 7 inch diameter cake tin and cook for 1$\frac{1}{2}$-2 hours in a moderate oven.

Alternative Flavourings

GINGER CAKE

Add 2 teaspoons ground ginger and $\frac{1}{4}$ teaspoon mixed spice with the flour.

PLAIN FRUIT

Add 4 oz. dried fruit and $\frac{1}{2}$ teaspoon mixed spice with the sugar.

CHOCOLATE

Add 3 tablespoons cocoa with the sugar.

ALL SPOONS ARE Level

CHOCOLATE PEPPERMINT PIE

6 oz. short crust pastry
4 tablespoons cornflour or
8 tablespoons flour
Pinch of salt
2 tablespoons cocoa

1 oz. sugar
1 pint milk
4 saccharin tablets
Vanilla essence

Line an 8 inc . flan tin with the pastry and bake it blind in a hot oven.
Mix the cornflour or flour, salt, cocoa and sugar with a little of the cold milk.
Boil the rest of the milk and dissolve the saccharin tablets in it. Add slowly to
the blended mixture and return to the pan. Bring to the boil stirring well and
boil for 5 minutes stirring all the time. Add the essence and whisk well. Pour
the mixture into the pastry case and when cool decorate with mock cream
flavoured with peppermint essence (see below).

MOCK CREAM

1 oz. margarine
1 oz. sugar
1 tablespoon household milk, dry

1 tablespoon warm water
Peppermint essence to taste

Cream margarine and sugar till white and smooth. Add the milk and water
gradually, beating well till quite smooth. Add a few drops of flavouring to
taste.

SULTANA PUDDING

8 oz. plain flour and
4 teaspoons baking powder or
8 oz. self-raising flour
Pinch of salt
1 tablespoon cocoa
1 teaspoon cinnamon
1 teaspoon spice

2 oz. cooking fat or suet
4 oz. sultanas
2 tablespoons syrup
½ teaspoon vanilla essence
6 saccharin tablets
About ¼ pint milk and water to mix

Mix the flour, baking powder if used, salt, cocoa, cinnamon and spice.
Rub in the fat or mix in the suet, add the sultanas. Add the syrup, vanilla
essence and crushed saccharin tablets
to the milk and water and use this to mix
the pudding to a dropping consistency.
Turn into a greased 2 pint size basin
and steam for 1½ hours.

SWEETENED CONDENSED Milk

Use this to save sugar in custards, sauces and all milk puddings. Dilute the milk according to the directions on the tin and then use as fresh milk.

CONDENSED MILK CAKE

3 oz. margarine
8 oz. self-raising flour or
8 oz. plain flour and
4 teaspoons baking powder
1 oz. sugar

3 oz. sultanas or raisins
1 tablespoon marmalade
3 tablespoons condensed milk
   made up to $\frac{1}{4}$ pint with water
2 beaten eggs, fresh or dried

Rub the margarine into the flour and add the baking powder if used, sugar and dried fruit. Mix to a soft consistency with the marmalade, milk and beaten eggs. Turn into a greased 6 inch cake tin and bake in a moderate oven for 45 minutes.

CREAMY FRUIT WHIP

$\frac{3}{4}$ pint thick fruit pulp or puree
   from bottled or fresh fruit

$\frac{1}{4}$ pint sweetened condensed
   milk

Mix the fruit pulp or puree with the condensed milk in a basin. Whisk for at least 10 minutes until light and frothing. Colour if necessary. Serve in individual glasses.

N.B.—A few drops of essence can be added for flavouring, e.g.: lemon essence with apples and almond essence with plums.

The Ministry of Food has compiled the " A.B.C. of Cookery " which gives suggestions and methods for cooking and preparing food. Obtainable from H.M. Stationery Office or through any Bookseller. Price 1/- or 1/2 by post.

Issued by the Ministry of Food   M. S. & H., Ltd. 51-2678 Dec., 1946 6492702

COOKING *for* ONE

FAT

1 Collect extra fat by trimming as much as possible from cooked and uncooked meat. Render it down and use as dripping.

2 The butter or margarine used for spreading may be extended by using the following recipe:—

> 4 oz. margarine or butter
> ½ tablespoon plain flour
> ½ teaspoon salt
> ¼ pint milk

Put 3 oz. margarine into a basin and cream with a wooden spoon. Melt 1 oz. in a saucepan, work in the flour and salt, and add the milk. Bring to the boil, stirring all the time, and boil gently for 5-7 minutes. Cool, and add to the margarine in the bowl. Mix well until smooth and allow to cool before using.

3 Always scrape the butter, margarine and cooking fat papers so as not to waste a scrap. Save the papers for greasing bowls or tins, for covering steamed puddings and for wrapping round cheese to keep it fresh.

4 If an oven or grill is available, bake or grill fish or meat cakes in preference to frying. This will save dripping for other purposes.

MINISTRY OF FOOD

LEAFLET

No. 31

SUGAR

1 Saccharin tablets may be used in place of sugar for sweetening 3-4 standard grain tablets being equivalent to 1 oz. sugar in sweetness.

2 The sugar ration may be extended by "fortifying" it with saccharin tablets. Crush 30 standard grain saccharin tablets with a rolling pin and mix with ½ lb. sugar; store in a covered jar. Less of this "fortified" sugar is required for sweetening purposes therefore use 1 oz. "fortified" sugar where recipes state that 2 oz. sugar is required; or if 1 teaspoonful of sugar is used for sweetening tea, use ½ teaspoonful of "fortified" sugar. ½ lb. "fortified" sugar is equivalent to 1 lb. sugar in sweetness.

MEAT BUYING

The cheaper cuts of meat such as shin of beef, stewing steak, neck of mutton, minced beef and breast of lamb or veal should be bought in preference to the more expensive cuts. Breast of lamb or veal can be stuffed and braised. If neck of mutton is bought, braise one chop (see recipe) and stew the remainder.

POINTS RATIONING

Sardines, ¼ lb. cans of household salmon (see recipes), brisling and cans of meat and vegetable stew are low in points and can be used for a main meal in place of meat.

Canned beans are useful by themselves or with meat to help stretch the ration. A packet of dried eggs will provide useful breakfast and supper dishes.

Dried fruit gives additional sweetness to cakes and puddings and cooked with fresh fruit it can take the place of some sugar.

Sweetened canned milk may be used in place of fresh milk for cooking and in beverages. It has the advantage of saving sugar and a can keeps several days after opening. Evaporated milk is useful but does not keep as long after being opened.

HOME-MADE STEAMERS

1 Use a flat sandwich tin which will fit into the top of a large saucepan. Punch holes all over it and use a cake tin or large basin, turned upside down, to cover it. The boiling water in the pan may be used for cooking vegetables or meat may be braised in the pan and a pudding steamed over it.

2 Use several small tins or jars with lids and stand these in a saucepan with the water half-way up their sides. Cook vegetables in the boiling water and potatoes in a cloth under the lid. Suitable foods for cooking in the tins or jars are:—stews, mince, meat or fish loaf, steamed puddings, milk puddings, soups, etc.

3 Steam fish fillets between two plates on top of a saucepan of boiling water. A pudding or vegetables or both can be cooked in the saucepan at the same time.

RECIPES

The cup used in these recipes is a ½-pint size, but any kind of jug or jar which holds a ½-pint will do. This can be checked by borrowing a ½-pint milk bottle and filling it with cold water. Tip this carefully into the jug or jar and mark the water level.

All the measures for cups and spoons are level. With all dry ingredients the cup or spoon should be filled and then levelled off with a knife. If the measures are heaped at all, the recipes will not turn out as well as they should.

BREAKFAST DISHES

PORRIDGE

2 tablespoons oatmeal	½ teaspoon salt
1 cup water	

Soak oatmeal in water overnight. In morning add salt, put in a saucepan. Bring to boil and boil 15-20 minutes.

N.B. When using rolled oats 3 tablespoons are required and it is not necessary to soak overnight.

STRETCHING THE BACON RATION

Eke out the bacon ration by serving it with fried, mashed or sliced potato; mixing a little chopped cooked bacon with mashed potatoes and form into cakes before frying or grilling; adding bacon to scrambled egg.

SAVOURY POTATO CAKES

2 tablespoons mashed potato	1 teaspoon chopped parsley
2 tablespoons cooked fish, flaked	½ teaspoon salt
	Pinch of pepper

Mix the ingredients well together. Turn on to a board and shape into 2 small cakes. Brown on both sides under the grill.

ALTERNATIVE FLAVOURINGS to use instead of fresh fish:—

1 1 tablespoon canned fish.

2 2 tablespoons grated cheese.

3 1½-2 tablespoons chopped cooked meat or sausage.

BEVERAGES

COCOA

2½ tablespoons household milk, dry	2-4 teaspoons cocoa
1 teaspoon sugar, or to taste	½ pint water

Mix the milk, sugar and cocoa to a smooth paste with a little of the water. Bring the remainder to the boil and add to the paste, stirring well. The flavour is greatly improved if the mixture is returned to the pan and allowed to boil for 1-2 minutes before serving.

To Make One Pint of BLACK COFFEE

2 tablespoons ground coffee.
½ pint freshly boiled water.

Place the coffee grounds in a jug and leave in a warm place for 10 minutes, cover with boiling water, stir well and leave standing for 15-20 minutes. Pour off carefully without disturbing the grounds at the bottom of jug. The coffee may need reheating before serving, but do not allow it to boil. Alternatively, stand the jug in boiling water while making the coffee.

To make WHITE COFFEE with very little milk

¼ pint black coffee   ¼ pint water
¼ pint milk (fresh or household)

Make the black coffee according to the recipe above. Keep hot. Mix the milk and water together, heat and serve in a jug.

MEAT AND FISH

CABBAGE AND MINCE SCRAMBLE

1½ dessertspoons fat (½ oz.)
2 cups shredded cabbage (6 oz.)
½ cup potatoes, thinly sliced (4 oz.)
2 teaspoons chopped leek or onion

3 tablespoons meat, minced or finely chopped (2 oz.)
½ teaspoon meat extract
2 tablespoons water
1 teaspoon salt
Pinch pepper

Make fat hot in frying-pan. Add cabbage, potatoes and leek or onion. Cook gently for 10 minutes, turning frequently without browning. Add meat, meat extract dissolved in the water and seasoning. Cover pan with plate or saucepan lid and simmer for 20-25 minutes. Stir to prevent sticking. Serve hot with a vegetable.

BRAISED LAMB CHOP

1 lamb chop
2 or 3 bacon rinds
¾ cup mixed vegetables, diced
1 tomato, if available
1 clove

2 or 3 peppercorns
1 or 2 leaves mint
1-1½ teaspoons salt
Pinch of pepper
½ cup stock or water

Trim all surplus fat from the chop. Heat the fat and bacon rinds in a pan to extract the fat and fry the chop until well browned on both sides. Remove the chop and pour off the fat. Place the vegetables in the pan with the tomato, spices, seasoning and stock or water. Place the chop on the vegetables, cover the pan with a lid and boil very gently for ¼-¾ hour. Remove the bacon rinds and serve the chop on a hot plate with the vegetables and gravy, which may be thickened with a little flour.

N.B. Small joints such as breast of mutton, loin or topside may be cooked in this manner. A breast should be boned and a layer of stuffing spread over it; it is then rolled up and tied or skewered into position.

Any meat left over may be treated in the same way as meat from a cold roast joint.

GRILLING

Grilling is the most economical way of cooking fillet steak and chops and a useful method for bacon, liver, kidneys, fish. Have the grill red hot and grease the grill rack before starting. Brush the food with melted fat (except fatty fish and bacon) and turn once or twice during cooking, being careful not to pierce it or the juices will run out.

ALLOW		
BACON	3-5 minutes	
BEEF STEAK	10-20 minutes,	depending on thickness and whether preferred under-done or well-done
FISH	5-20 minutes,	depending on size and thickness
FISH CAKES AND RISSOLES	5-10 minutes	
KIDNEYS	6-10 minutes	
LIVER	5-10 minutes,	according to thickness
MUTTON CHOPS	10-20 minutes	
MUTTON CUTLETS	7-10 minutes	
PORK OR VEAL CHOPS	20 minutes	
SAUSAGES	9-12 minutes	

CREAMED SALMON

1 tablespoon flour
½ teaspoon salt
Pinch of pepper
Pinch of mustard
4 tablespoons water

1 teaspoon vinegar
½ tin household salmon (½ lb. size)
1 tablespoon chopped parsley

Blend the flour and seasonings with the water and bring to the boil, stirring all the time. Boil gently for 3 minutes, then beat in the vinegar and salmon and cook over a low heat for 5 minutes. Add the parsley and serve hot on toast, or cold with salad.

N.B. Use the remaining salmon to make a salad or fish pie or fish cakes.

VEGETABLES and SALADS

ROOT VEGETABLES

Scrub well, peel thinly or scrape and cut into slices or dice. Cook in a very little boiling salted water, with a lid on the pan, for about 20 minutes or until tender. Drain and serve. The liquid in which the vegetables are cooked should be kept for using in stews, soups and sauces. Raw grated vegetables such as turnip, swede, carrot, beetroot, etc., can be used in salads.

ALL SPOONS ARE LEVEL   ALL RECIPES FOR ONE PERSON.

POTATOES

Scrub well and cook in a little boiling salted water, with a lid on the pan, until tender. Drain well and shake the potatoes in the pan over a low heat for a minute or two; this dries the potatoes and leaves them floury. Peel before serving if liked.

Cook rather more potatoes than are required for one meal. Those left over can be used to eke out the bacon for breakfast, cubed and used in salads, or mashed and mixed with fish or cooked meat for fish cakes and rissoles.

GREEN VEGETABLES

Use as fresh as possible. Wash well and remove any coarse or withered outer leaves. Shred and cook in a very little boiling salted water, with a lid on the pan, for 10-15 minutes. Strain, saving the liquid, and serve at once. Spinach does not require any water and need not be shredded.

Remove any decayed leaves from Brussels sprouts and wash well. Cut very large sprouts in half and cook as above. Break cauliflower and broccoli into sprigs and wash well. Cook as above. The green leaves may be cooked in the same way as cabbage.

Use finely shredded raw cabbage heart, savoy, spinach, sprouts, chopped cauliflower, watercress, etc., in salads.

INDIVIDUAL SALAD

4-5 tablespoons grated raw carrot
½ cup chopped or grated apple
2 tablespoons raisins or other dried fruit

3-4 curly lettuce leaves
1 tablespoon thick salad dressing

Mix the carrot, apple and raisins together, keeping 2 or 3 raisins to garnish the top. Heap it in a nest of lettuce leaves. Garnish with salad dressing and raisins.

The filling may be varied, using other fruit and vegetables such as pears, prunes, plums, swede, spinach, cucumber, celery and tomatoes.

HORS D'OEUVRE SALAD

2-3 sardines
2-3 lettuce leaves
3 tablespoons raw turnip, grated

3 tablespoons cooked beans
3 tablespoons cooked beetroot, chopped
Finely grated cheese

Place the sardines on the lettuce leaves. Arrange the other ingredients in heaps around this and garnish with finely grated cheese.

COLE SLAW

1 cup finely shredded cabbage heart or sprouts
1 small onion, chopped finely
1-2 tablespoons salad dressing

Mix all the ingredients together and serve as accompaniment to hot or cold meat or fish in place of a cooked vegetable.

SWEET DISHES

STEAMED PUDDING

6 tablespoons plain flour and
1 teaspoon baking powder or
6 tablespoons self-raising flour
Pinch of salt
1 tablespoon margarine or
    cooking fat

1 tablespoon sugar
Few drops of flavouring
3 tablespoons milk or water
    to mix

Mix flour, baking powder if used, and salt. Rub in the margarine or fat and add the sugar. Mix with the flavouring and milk or water, turn into a greased ¼ pint basin, or 2 small moulds, and steam for 30-35 minutes. Serve with any sweet sauce. The remainder of the pudding may be eaten cold or reheated.

THIS RECIPE MAY BE VARIED AS FOLLOWS:

1 FRUIT PUDDING — Add 2-3 tablespoons dried fruit with the sugar.

2 CHOCOLATE PUDDING — Add ½ tablespoon cocoa and ½ tablespoon sugar to the dry ingredients

3 GINGER OR SPICE PUDDING — Add 1 teaspoon ground ginger or mixed spice to the dry ingredients

4 JAM PUDDING — Place 1 tablespoon jam at the bottom of the basin before adding the pudding mixture

FRUIT WHIP

1½ tablespoons semolina
1 cup fruit juice or puree

1 tablespoon sugar

Blend semolina with a little of the fruit juice. Bring the remainder to the boil. Pour on to the blended mixture and return to pan. Stir over gentle heat, allow to boil 7-10 minutes to cook the semolina. Sweeten to taste. Turn into a bowl and allow to cool. When cold, but not set, whisk thoroughly till light and fluffy. Serve cold.

ORANGE OR LEMON WHIP

1 tablespoon cornflour or
2 tablespoons plain flour
½ tablespoon sugar

2 tablespoons lemon or orange
squash made up to ½ cup
with water

Mix the dry ingredients to a smooth paste with a little of the liquid. Bring the remainder to the boil and pour on to the blended mixture. Return to the pan, bring to the boil and boil gently for 5 minutes, stirring frequently. Leave to cool, then whisk until light and frothy. Serve very cold.

SUPPER DISHES

FRENCH PEASANT SOUP

¾ cup mixed vegetables
(carrots, parsnips, potatoes,
etc.)
1 cup boiling stock or water
1 teaspoon salt

2-3 tablespoons breadcrumbs
Pinch of pepper
2 tablespoons chopped parsley
½-1 oz. grated cheese

Prepare and slice or dice the vegetables, place in the stock or water to which the salt has been added. Boil gently until tender, about 20 minutes. Add the breadcrumbs and simmer for a few minutes. Mash well, season and add the parsley and cheese just before serving.

SAUSAGE DUMPLINGS

6 tablespoons plain flour and
1 teaspoon baking powder or
6 tablespoons self-raising flour
Pinch of salt
Pinch of pepper
2 tablespoons chopped cooked
sausage or liver or breakfast sausage

2 tablespoons milk
to mix
1 teaspoon meat or vegetable
extract
½ cup boiling water

Mix the dry ingredients together, add the sausage and mix to a soft dough with milk or water. Form into 2 dumplings. Add the extract to the water and, when dissolved, add the dumplings. Boil for 15 minutes. Serve hot with the gravy.

PAN HASH

½ rasher bacon, chopped
2 tablespoons mashed potato
2 tablespoons chopped cooked
vegetables

½ teaspoon salt
Pinch of pepper
A little fat for frying, if
necessary

Fry the bacon until crisp, remove from the pan and mix with the potato, vegetables and seasoning. Fry the mixture in the bacon fat until well-browned about 10 minutes.

N.B. If no cooked vegetables are available, 4 tablespoons mashed potato may be used.

ALTERNATIVE FLAVOURINGS to use instead of bacon:—

1 1 tablespoon chopped cooked meat.

2 1 tablespoon flaked cooked fish, or canned fish.

SAVOURY SPROUTS

½ lb. sprouts
1½ tablespoons flour
½ cup vegetable water and
milk

3 tablespoons grated cheese
Few drops lemon essence
½ teaspoon salt
Pinch pepper

Prepare the sprouts and cook in a little boiling salted water until tender; drain and keep hot, saving the liquid. Blend the flour with a little of the liquid, bring the remainder to the boil and pour on to the blended flour. Return to the pan; bring to the boil, stirring all the time, and boil gently for 5 minutes. Add the cheese, a few drops of lemon essence and season well. Add the sprouts, reheat and serve very hot.

SARDINES & CURRY SAUCE

½-1 teaspoon curry powder
1-2 spring onions, chopped
finely
1 teaspoon cooking fat or
dripping
1 tablespoon flour

4 tablespoons water
½ teaspoon salt
Few drops of vinegar
½ can sardines (4½ oz. size)
1 round of toast

Fry the curry powder and onion in the fat for a few minutes. Work in the flour, add the water gradually and bring to the boil, stirring all the time. Boil gently for 5 minutes and add the salt and a few drops of vinegar. Place the sardines on the toast, pour over the curry sauce and serve at once.

N.B. The remainder of the sardines can be used for sandwiches or in a salad.

A SALAD a day
all the year round

GREEN LEAF VEGETABLES

At least one of these should be included in every salad : raw cabbage heart, savoy, spinach, sprouts, young leaves of kale and young turnip tops, watercress including the stalks, lettuce and endive.

ROOT VEGETABLES

Raw or cooked beetroot, turnip, parsnip, carrot, kohlrabi, swede.

OTHER VEGETABLES

Cooked potato, raw radishes, cucumber, onions, leeks ; cooked or raw peas, cooked french or runner beans, celery, shallots, chicory cauliflower, broccoli and cooked broad beans.

FLAVOURINGS

Green herbs, chives, parsley, mint, green tops of leeks and spring onions, young celery leaves, nasturtium and dandelion leaves, mustard and cress, garlic.

FRUIT

Any fruit, fresh or dried.

MEAT & FISH

Cooked or canned, any kind is suitable.

EGGS

Fresh or dried may be used. Serve either as scrambled or hard boiled.

CHEESE

Any kind is suitable, either grated or cut in cubes or slices.

MINISTRY OF FOOD COOKERY LEAFLET NUMBER 12

A CRISP, FRESH SALAD WILL BRING EXTRA NOURISHMENT TO YOUR MEALS

DURING the past few years we have discovered how good a daily green salad can be. People who tell you that they feel much better now that they eat salads are not just food faddists. They are stating a fact that has been proved over and over again. We know now that many vegetables contain more vitamin C than some fruits and, in addition, mineral salts which are essential to health.

A good salad does not consist of a lettuce leaf and a radish or two. If you look at the list of suitable ingredients on the first page of this leaflet you will see how great a variety there is from which to choose. Clever mixing can give you a different salad every day.

WAYS OF SERVING SALADS

1. Serve a small helping with hot meat, fish or other savoury dish. For this use a few sprigs of watercress or a little raw shredded cabbage or a mixed green salad. Most people will prefer no dressing with it.

2. Use raw vegetable salad as a filling for sandwiches, rolls and scones. The salad can either be used alone, in which case a little dressing is an improvement, or added to egg, cheese, fish or meat fillings.

3. Salads served as a separate course can come either at the beginning of a meal in place of soup, such as the hors d'oeuvre type of salad or as a course to follow the meat and vegetables, perhaps in place of a sweet course. A good kind to use for this is the individual salad, that is, one helping arranged attractively on each plate.

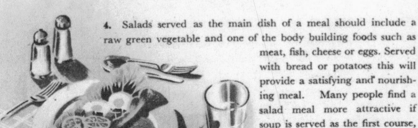

4. Salads served as the main dish of a meal should include a raw green vegetable and one of the body building foods such as meat, fish, cheese or eggs. Served with bread or potatoes this will provide a satisfying and nourishing meal. Many people find a salad meal more attractive if soup is served as the first course, or if a hot sweet is served afterwards.

TIPS FOR SALAD MAKERS

1. When making salads touch the leaves as little as possible. Use directly after picking or buying. If this is not convenient a saucepan with a well-fitting lid placed on a cool floor is excellent for keeping salad vegetables crisp.

2. Just before serving, wash the leaves carefully, shake off the water gently and dry by swinging in a clean cloth or in a wire salad basket if you have one. Outside leaves should be saved for soup.

3. Shred raw green vegetables with a sharp knife. Parsley should be coarsely chopped.

4. Root vegetables such as carrots should be washed and scraped lightly, then shredded or grated. Alternatively, they may be cooked and chopped or sliced when cold. Potatoes should be used cooked and cold. The thick skins of turnips and swedes should be removed by peeling.

5. Be sure the salad is well flavoured. See " Flavourings."

6. Add colour to the salad by using raw grated carrot, beetroot, swede, whole or sliced tomato, radishes or hard boiled eggs.

7. Serve as soon as possible after preparation.

8. If a salad is served as a main meal or as the only green vegetable, provide at least 3 oz. (i.e., one or two cups) of raw vegetables per person. At least half of this should be green vegetables.

RECIPES

All quantities for four unless otherwise stated. All measures level. The cup used holds ½ pint. Vegetables and fruit in the recipes are raw unless otherwise stated.

COLE SLAW

4 cups shredded cabbage heart
3 tablespoons chopped spring
    onions

8-10 tablespoons salad dressing
    (about ¼ pint)

Wash the cabbage and shred finely. Put into basin and add chopped onion and salad dressing. Mix well and turn into a salad bowl to serve. Chopped chives may be used instead of onions or the bowl can be rubbed with garlic before the cabbage is placed in it.

POTATO SALAD

1½ lb. potatoes
¼ pint salad dressing

1 tablespoon chopped chives
1 tablespoon chopped mint

Scrub potatoes and boil until tender. Peel while still warm and cut into large dice. Mix with salad dressing and herbs and place in salad bowl. Serve cold.

MIXED VEGETABLE SALAD

1 cup cooked peas (fresh or dried)
1 cup cooked chopped beetroot
1 cup grated carrot

½ cup grated turnip
1½ cups shredded cabbage
1 tablespoon coarsely chopped
    fresh herbs

The vegetables can be arranged in strips on an oval dish, e.g., cabbage, beetroot, turnip, carrot, peas, or mixed together in a bowl with salad dressing. Garnish with mixed herbs, e.g., nasturtium leaves, parsley, mint, dandelion leaves, watercress.

INDIVIDUAL SALAD

6 tablespoons grated carrot
6 tablespoons chopped or grated apple
2 tablespoons raisins or other
    dried fruit

3-4 curly lettuce leaves
1 tablespoon thick salad dressing

Mix carrot, apple, and raisins together, keeping two or three raisins to decorate the top. Heap in a nest of lettuce leaves. Garnish with salad dressing and a few raisins. The filling may be varied, using other fruit and vegetables, such as pears, prunes, plums, swede, spinach, cucumber, celery and tomatoes.

CABBAGE AND FRUIT SALAD

3 cups finely shredded cabbage
1 cup chopped apple
½ cup chopped ripe pear
1 tablespoon finely chopped onion
½ cup grated carrot
1 dessertspoon chopped mint
3-4 tablespoons salad dressing
Salt and pepper

Mix together the cabbage, apple, pear, onion, carrot and mint. Moisten with the salad dressing and add a little salt and pepper if necessary. Pile on to a dish and garnish with small sprigs of mint.

CELERY, BEETROOT AND BLANCHED CABBAGE

1-1½ lb. cabbage
1 pint boiling water
1 cup shredded beetroot
1 cup finely sliced celery

1 tablespoon finely chopped onion
  or leek
Salt and pepper

Shred the cabbage, add to the boiling water and boil for 2 minutes. Drain and arrange round a dish forming a border. Mix together the beetroot, celery and onion or leek, seasoning well. Pile in the centre of the dish and serve with dressing handed separately.

MAIN MEAL SALADS

FISH SALAD

1 cup chopped spinach
1½ cups grated carrot
1 cup sliced cauliflower

4 pilchards
Salad dressing
A few sprigs of cauliflower

Mix spinach, carrot and cauliflower together and place in bowl. Lay fish on top and decorate with salad dressing and sprigs of cauliflower.
Soused herrings, mackerel or sardines may be used instead of pilchards.

EGG AND CABBAGE SALAD

4 hard boiled eggs (fresh or
  dried)
4 cups finely shredded cabbage
1 cup chopped watercress

¼ pint salad dressing
1 large tomato
¼ cup chopped cooked beetroot

Chop up three eggs into small dice and mix with cabbage, cress and salad dressing. Place in salad bowl and decorate with the remaining egg, tomato and beetroot.

HORS D'OEUVRE SALAD *(Individual helping)*

1 dried egg (scrambled)
1 teaspoon chopped herbs
2-3 lettuce leaves
2 tablespoons chopped cooked beetroot
1 sardine

Radish rose
2 tablespoons raw grated turnip
3 tablespoons cooked beans
2 tablespoons finely grated cheese

The scrambled egg is mixed with the herbs and placed on the lettuce leaves. The other ingredients are arranged in heaps round this.
This may also be served in an hors d'oeuvres dish. Other cooked or raw vegetables, mixed pickles and tomato roses may be used as alternatives in the above recipe.

SAUSAGE AND POTATO SALAD

1-1½ lb. cooked diced potato
4 cold boiled sausages
2-3 tablespoons chopped pickle
Salad dressing to moisten (about
  4 tablespoons)
½ cup cooked peas
¼ cup cooked diced beetroot
12-16 radishes

Mix potato, sausage and chopped pickle with salad dressing. Place in salad bowl and decorate with peas, beetroot and radish.

★ SALAD  DRESSINGS

THIN SALAD DRESSING

(For use in place of oil and vinegar dressing).

½ teaspoon mustard
½ teaspoon salt
1 teaspoon sugar

Pinch of pepper
2 tablespoons top of milk
1 tablespoon vinegar

Mix the seasoning together and mix in the milk gradually. When quite smooth, add the vinegar and stir well. Use the same day.

ECONOMICAL SALAD DRESSING

2 oz. flour
1 tablespoon sugar
2 teaspoons mustard
2 teaspoons salt

¼ teaspoon pepper
1 pint milk or milk and vegetable water
4 tablespoons vinegar

Mix dry ingredients together and blend with a little milk. Boil the rest of the milk and pour on to blended flour. Return to saucepan, stir until boiling and boil for five minutes. Whisk in vinegar.

CREAMY SALAD DRESSING

2 tablespoons flour
1 tablespoon dried egg, dry
1 teaspoon mustard
1 teaspoon sugar
1 teaspoon salt

Pepper
½ pint milk or vegetable water
1 oz. margarine
4 tablespoons vinegar

Mix the flour, egg, mustard, sugar, salt and pepper. Mix to a smooth paste with a little of the milk or vegetable water. Boil remaining liquid, pour on to the blended flour, return to pan and bring to the boil. Boil five minutes stirring well. Remove from heat and add margarine. Mix well and add vinegar.

Some of these recipes are demonstrated in the film " Salads," made by the Ministry of Information.

The Ministry of Food has compiled the ABC of Cookery, which gives suggestions for cooking and preparing foods. Obtainable from H.M. Stationery Office. Price 1s. 0d. or by post: 1s. 2d.

Issued by the Ministry of Food
Revised and Reprinted October 1946

64105810

SUGGESTIONS *for*

BREAKFAST

A GOOD BREAKFAST EVERY DAY IS THE FIRST RULE IN THE BOOK OF HEALTH

Get up early enough to enjoy breakfast without hurry. A cup of tea and a morsel of toast gulped down with one eye on the clock is no use to anyone. Breakfast is an important meal for all of us, but especially important for growing school children and young factory workers.

MINISTRY OF FOOD LEAFLET No. 33

BREAKFAST MENU

PORRIDGE
(or other cereal with fruit or milk)

COOKED DISH

(Bacon or fish or meat or cheese or egg with fried potatoes
or fried bread)

NATIONAL or WHOLEMEAL BREAD
with
BUTTER or MARGARINE
and
MARMALADE or JAM or other SWEET SPREAD
TEA or COFFEE
COCOA or MILK for children

RECIPES

PORRIDGE (I)

4–6 oz oatmeal   *1 teaspoon salt*
2 pints water

Soak the oatmeal in the water overnight. Next morning, add salt, bring to the boil and cook for 15–20 minutes, stirring occasionally to prevent sticking.

N.B.—If thick porridge is preferred, use the larger amount of oatmeal.

PORRIDGE (II)

6–8 oz. rolled oats or barley flakes   *1 teaspoon salt*
2 pints water

Mix the rolled oats or barley flakes with a little of the cold water. Boil the rest and pour on to the oats or flakes stirring well. Return to the pan. Add the salt and boil the porridge for 5–10 minutes, stirring at intervals.

N.B.—If thick porridge is preferred use the larger amounts of rolled oats or barley flakes.

SEMOLINA PORRIDGE

4–6 oz. semolina
2 pints liquid (1 pint or less milk and
    remainder in water)

1 teaspoon salt

Blend the semolina and salt with a little of the cold liquid. Bring the remainder to the boil and pour on to the blended semolina. Return to the pan and boil gently for 15–20 minutes stirring well to prevent it burning.

N.B.— If thick porridge is preferred use the larger amount of semolina.

WHEATMEALIES

Cut bread into small dice not more than ¼" thick. Spread on a flat tin and bake until quite crisp. Serve with milk and sugar or with stewed fruit.

SUMMER BREAKFAST DISH

4 oz. rolled oats or barley flakes or kernels
4 tablespoons milk

½–¾ lb. grated apple
1–2 tablespoons sugar

Soak the rolled oats or barley flakes or kernels overnight in barely enough water to cover. In the morning, beat up well with the other ingredients. This is a delicious alternative to porridge on summer mornings.

FRIED BREAD and BACON

4 rashers bacon
4 slices bread ½" thick (from a 1 lb. loaf)

Fat for frying, if necessary

Fry the bacon and push to one side or remove from the pan and keep hot. If the bacon is lean it may be necessary to add a little extra fat to have enough to cover the bottom of the pan. Fry the slices of bread in the hot fat until golden brown on both sides. Serve with the bacon.

BACON TURNOVERS

1–2 rashers fat bacon
4 oz. plain flour with
2 teaspoons baking powder
or 4 oz. self-raising flour

½ teaspoon salt
½–1 teaspoon mixed herbs
4–6 tablespoons milk

Fry and chop the bacon, keeping the fat to fry the turnover. Mix the dry ingredients to a scone dough with milk and roll to ¼" thickness. Cut into eight 3" rounds and place bacon in the centre of four. Damp edges and cover with remaining four rounds. Fry in the bacon fat for about 10 minutes until cooked through and golden brown on both sides.

FRITTERS

4 oz. self-raising flour
or 4 oz. plain flour and
2 teaspoons baking powder
1 teaspoon salt

½ teaspoon pepper
¼ pint milk (approx.)
2 oz. chopped bacon
Fat for frying

Mix flour, baking powder, if used, salt and pepper well together.   Mix to a stiff batter with the milk.   Beat well. Add the chopped bacon.   Fry tablespoons of the mixture in hot fat until golden brown on both sides.   Serve at once. This quantity makes about 8 fritters.

ALTERNATIVE FLAVOURINGS TO USE INSTEAD OF THE BACON:—

1.   2 oz. grated cheese
2.   2–3 oz. finely chopped cooked meat.
3.   2–3 oz. flaked cooked fish and 1 tablespoon chopped parsley
4.   ½ tin (4½ oz. size) mashed sardines and 1 dessertspoon vinegar

SAVOURY POTATO CAKES

8 oz. mashed potato
8 oz. cooked fish, flaked
1 tablespoon chopped parsley

1 teaspoon salt
¼ teaspoon pepper

Mix all the ingredients well together.   Turn on to a board and shape into 4 cakes. Brown under the grill on both sides or bake in a moderate oven till firm and brown.

ALTERNATIVE FLAVOURINGS TO USE INSTEAD OF THE FRESH FISH:—

1.   **CANNED FISH.**   Use 2 oz. sardines, mackerel, pilchards or herrings.
2.   **BACON.**   Omit the salt.   Use 2 oz. chopped bacon.   Fry the bacon before mixing with the other ingredients.   Use the bacon fat for frying the potato cakes.
3.   **CHEESE AND PARSLEY.**   Use only ½ teaspoon salt.   Add 1½ oz. grated cheese and 1 tablespoon chopped parsley.
4.   **MEAT.**   Use 2 oz. cooked meat, minced or finely chopped and add 1 teaspoon Worcester sauce.

PAN HASH

8 oz. cooked mashed potatoes
8 oz. mixed cooked vegetables, chopped
2 oz. chopped cooked bacon

Salt and pepper
1 oz. fat for frying (use the bacon fat)

Mix all the ingredients together.   Melt the fat in a frying pan and fry the mixture on both sides till well browned, about 15 minutes.

NOTE.—If no cooked vegetables are available, 1 lb. cooked mashed potatoes may be used.

ALTERNATIVE FLAVOURINGS TO USE INSTEAD OF THE BACON:—

1.   2 oz. grated cheese
2.   2 oz. chopped cooked meat
3.   2 oz. flaked cooked fish

POTATO PUFFS

PUFFS
1 lb. cooked mashed potato
Salt and pepper
A little flour

FILLINGS
6 oz. cooked sausage meat, or
6 oz. cooked root vegetables, chopped
and 1 oz. grated cheese

Mix cold mashed potato with seasoning. Add enough flour to bind the potatoes into a dough which will roll out easily, roll out, cut into four fairly large rounds. Season the filling chosen and place a little on each round, damp edges, fold over and seal. Bake on greased tray or fry in shallow fat.

CHEESE and VEGETABLE CUTLETS

4 oz. grated cheese
8 oz. mashed potatoes
4 oz. cooked peas
2 carrots, finely grated
1 onion, chopped finely

4 tablespoons flour
Salt and pepper
Browned breadcrumbs

Mix together the cheese, vegetables, and flour, and season well. Form into eight cutlets and coat with browned breadcrumbs. Bake in a moderate oven for 20–25 minutes, or fry in a little fat for 5 minutes, or grill until brown on both sides.

FRIED CHEESE SANDWICHES

2 oz. cheese, sliced
4 slices of bread from a 2 lb. loaf

¼ teaspoon made mustard
Fat for frying

Place the cheese on two of the slices of bread and lightly spread with the mustard. Cover with the remaining slices of bread, cut in two, and fry in hot fat till golden brown on both sides. Serve hot.

POTATO FADGE with FRIED BACON

8 oz. cooked mashed potato
Salt and pepper

1–2 oz. flour
4 rashers bacon

Mix potato, seasoning and enough flour to make a stiff dough. Roll out ¼ inch thick and cut into eight pieces. Fry bacon and keep hot, then fry the fadge in the bacon fat until brown on both sides. Serve with the bacon.

FRIED HERRINGS

4 filleted, or whole herrings
3 tablespoons flour, or oatmeal
2 teaspoons salt

A little pepper
Fat for frying

Wipe the fish and dip it in the flour or oatmeal to which the salt and pepper have been added. Heat a little fat in a frying pan until a faint blue haze rises. Put in the fish, and cook until brown on both sides.

N.B.—If whole herrings are used be sure they are cleaned before cooking.

POACHED KIPPERS

Cut off the heads and tails. Put the fish in a frying pan with just enough cold water to cover. Bring to the boil, simmer for a few minutes. Drain well and serve with a small knob of butter or margarine on each kipper.

When available, smoked haddock can also be cooked in this way.

GRILLED FISH

1 tablespoon flour	2 tablespoons milk
½ teaspoon salt	1 lb. fillet of fish, cut in pieces,
Pinch of pepper	Browned breadcrumbs
Pinch of grated nutmeg	1 oz. cooking fat or dripping

Blend the flour, salt, pepper and nutmeg with the milk. Dip the pieces of fish in this and then roll in browned crumbs. Heat the fat in the grill pan and, when hot, dip the fish in it and grill on both sides till brown and cooked. The pieces of coated fish can be baked in a hot oven for ½ hour. Cook in a baking tin or shallow fireproof dish with the fat.

NOTE.—The pieces of fish can be sprinkled with salt and pepper and coated in breadcrumbs only.

HERRING ROE SAVOURY

8 soft roes	1½ tablespoons flour
¼ pint milk	Salt and pepper
4 slices of toast	Chopped parsley

Rinse roes. Stew in the milk until they are tender about 10-15 minutes. Place 2 roes on each piece of toast and keep hot. Mix the flour to a smooth paste with a little cold water, add the boiled milk. Return to the saucepan and stir until boiling. Boil 5 minutes, season well, and pour over the roes. Garnish with chopped parsley.

HARD ROES

These may be washed, dipped in flour or egg and breadcrumbs, and fried in a little hot fat till golden brown.

GRILLED PILCHARDS on TOAST

1 tin of pilchards (15 oz. size)	4 slices of buttered toast

Divide the pilchards on to the four slices of toast and place under the grill for several minutes to heat.

FRIED PILCHARDS on FRIED BREAD

1 tin pilchards (15 oz. size)	Fat for frying, if necessary
4 slices of bread	

Fry the pilchards till brown on both sides. They should be sufficiently oily to fry without extra fat. Remove from the pan and keep hot. Add a little extra fat if necessary to fry the slices of bread till golden brown on both sides. Divide the pilchards on to the four slices of fried bread and serve hot.

N.B.—Canned herrings or sardines may be used instead of pilchards in either of the recipes above.

Issued by the Ministry of Food

W.H.& S. 51-2430

64102108

Easy to make
SOUPS AND BROTHS

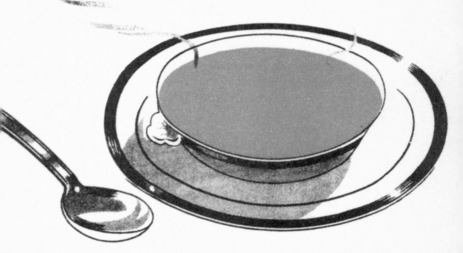

Once upon a time cooks used to think a good soup needed 3 or 4 hours cooking, and that to be nourishing it must be made from meat and bones. To-day we know better. We know that, although meat and bone stocks are tasty, they have very little food value because only the flavour of the meat comes out in the soup. We know, too, that tasty soups can be made quickly using vegetables and vegetable water or stock from meat cubes or vegetable extract. These soups may be made nourishing and sustaining by adding body building food such as milk, cheese, eggs, fish and meat. Broth is a soup of this kind and is popular with the North Country housewife who prefers to cook some of her meat ration in this way and serve it in place of a meat dish.

MINISTRY OF FOOD

M of F

LEAFLET

No. 15

1 For a mid-morning or late evening snack.
Any of the vegetable or cream soups are suitable.

2 As an appetiser at the beginning of dinner.
This should be only a light vegetable soup. Do not serve a large portion or the appetite will be spoilt for the main dish that follows.

3 As a main dish. This soup should contain one of the body building foods such as meat, fish, eggs or cheese. Examples are the recipes for fish soup, Scotch broth, and vegetable broth with dumplings. Alternatively for supper or lunch serve a vegetable soup first and follow this with a salad or savoury dish containing one of the body building foods.

STOCK FOR SOUPS

It is not necessary to have meat or bone stock to make good soups. Vegetable stock or vegetable water left over after cooking vegetables gives an excellent flavour to any soup, and in addition contains valuable protective substances.

To make vegetable stock use the outside leaves and stalks of cabbage, outside stalks of celery, cauliflower stalks, watercress stalks, etc., as well as whole vegetables. Chop or shred the vegetables and put them in enough boiling water to cover. Boil for about half an hour. Strain before using.

For a quickly made stock dissolve some meat or yeast extract in boiling water.

Remember that stock does not keep very long, especially in hot weather, so be sure to use it up quickly. Do not leave it standing in the saucepan. Empty it into a clean jug or basin.

Many of the recipes which follow give alternatives of stock or water. It is worth while taking the trouble to use stock, which gives a better flavour to the soup.

3

VEGETABLE SOUP

¾ lb. mixed vegetables (including
  some onion and some green
  vegetables)
½ oz. cooking fat or dripping·
1½ pints stock or water

3 teaspoons salt
Good pinch of pepper
3-4 tablespoons grated cheese
  (optional)

Prepare and shred or slice the vegetables. Heat the fat or dripping and add the vegetables. Cover with a lid and cook gently without browning for 15 to 20 minutes, shaking the pan occasionally to prevent sticking. Add the liquid and seasoning and boil gently until the vegetables are tender. For variety 1 oz. of macaroni, spaghetti, or noodles, may be added with the liquid. Serve the cheese separately to be sprinkled on the soup according to taste.

TOMATO SOUP

½ oz. cooking fat or dripping
3 oz. carrot, sliced
4 oz. potato, sliced
Piece of leek or celery, sliced
2 or 3 bacon rinds

2 pints boiling stock or water
1 lb. fresh or canned tomatoes
1 tablespoon salt
¼ teaspoon pepper
2 oz. flour

Heat the fat or dripping in a saucepan and fry the carrot, potato, leek or celery and bacon rinds for a few minutes. Pour on the boiling stock or water, add the sliced tomatoes and seasoning and boil gently until the vegetables are tender. Remove the bacon rinds and mash with a wooden spoon, or put through a sieve. Thicken with the flour, blended with a little cold stock or water. If it can be spared, a tablespoon of sugar improves the flavour of this soup.

BEETROOT and CABBAGE SOUP

2 pints water
1 lb. raw beetroot, grated coarsely
½ lb. cabbage, shredded
Salt and pepper
2 teaspoons vinegar

2 cloves
3 tablespoons flour
A little grated cheese
Chopped parsley

Bring the water to the boil, add the beetroot and boil gently for 10 minutes. Add the cabbage and season well, adding the vinegar and cloves Cover the pan and boil gently until tender, about 15 minutes. Blend the flour with a little cold water and stir it into the soup. Boil 5 minutes. Serve sprinkled with grated cheese and chopped parsley.

FRENCH PEASANT SOUP

2 pints vegetable stock or water
1 lb. mixed root vegetables, diced
  (including potatoes)
1 tablespoon salt
¼ teaspoon pepper

2 oz. stale breadcrumbs
2 oz. grated cheese
2 tablespoons coarsely chopped
  parsley

Bring the stock or water to the boil and add the diced vegetables, salt and pepper. Boil gently until tender, and stir in the breadcrumbs, grated cheese and parsley. Serve at once.

PARSNIP or SWEDE SOUP

2 pints water or stock
1½ lb. parsnips or swedes, peeled and shredded
2 oz. leek or onion

Salt and pepper
2 tablespoons flour
4 tablespoons milk
2 tablespoons chopped parsley

Put water or stock in a pan and bring to boil. When boiling add shredded parsnips or swedes, chopped leek or onion and seasoning. Boil for 20 minutes. Mix flour to a smooth paste with a little water. Add to soup, reboil, stirring to prevent lumps. Cook for 5 minutes. Add milk and reheat but do not reboil. Stir in coarsely chopped parsley just before serving.

CHEESE and POTATO SOUP

1½ lb. potatoes
1 stick celery
3 oz. onion or leek
2 pints vegetable stock or water

1 oz. flour
2 oz. grated cheese
2 tablespoons chopped parsley

Scrub and slice potatoes and celery. Peel and slice onion or leek. Place vegetables in boiling water or stock. Cook with the lid on till quite soft. Rub through a sieve or mash well with a wooden spoon. Blend the flour with a little water. Add to the soup, bring to the boil again, and boil 5 minutes. Add the cheese and parsley and serve.

KALE and POTATO SOUP

2 pints stock or water
1½ lb. potatoes peeled and chopped
3 oz. onion or leek, chopped
4 oz. kale, shredded

4 tablespoons household milk, dry
Salt and pepper
Chopped parsley

Boil half the stock or water and add the potatoes and onion or leek. Boil until the vegetables are soft, then mash. Bring to the boil again and add the washed and shredded kale. Cook for a further half hour. Mix the milk with the rest of the water and add; reheat. Season with salt and pepper and sprinkle with chopped parsley before serving.

CABBAGE SOUP

1 oz. dripping or cooking fat
4 oz. shredded cabbage
1 medium sized onion, chopped
3 oz. carrot, grated
1 oz. oatmeal

1 pint stock or water
2 teaspoons salt
Pinch of pepper
1 pint milk

Melt the dripping or fat in a saucepan and fry the vegetables gently for about 5 minutes, without browning. Add the cabbage and oatmeal and cook for a further 3 minutes. Add the stock or water and seasoning. Boil gently for 20 minutes. Lastly, add the milk and reheat.
NOTE.—Any vegetable can be used instead of the cabbage, according to the season, e.g., beetroot, artichoke, etc.

ALL SPOONS ARE LEVEL - ALL RECIPES FOR 4 PERSONS

WATERCRESS SOUP

½ oz. cooking fat or dripping
4 oz. leek, sliced
1 oz. watercress, chopped
1 lb. potatoes, cut in quarters
1 pint of water

2 teaspoons salt
¼ teaspoon pepper
2 or 3 bacon rinds
½ pint milk

Heat the fat or dripping in a pan and add the sliced leek, half the watercress and the potatoes. Fry gently without browning for about 5 minutes. Add the water, salt, pepper and bacon rinds. Boil gently until the potatoes are soft, then mash with a wooden spoon. Remove bacon rinds; add the milk and, just before serving, the remainder of the watercress.

VEGETABLE PUREE FOR CREAM SOUPS

To obtain ½ pint vegetable puree use one of the following:—
1 lb. any root vegetable
or ¾ lb. potatoes and ½ lb. watercress
or ¾ lb. tomatoes

or 2 lb. marrow or cucumber
or 6 oz. dried peas

Whichever vegetable is used cook it until tender in ½ pint boiling salted water. The dried peas should be soaked overnight before cooking. Rub the cooked vegetables through a sieve and keep hot until required. If not quite ½ pint puree is obtained make it up with hot water.

CREAM OF VEGETABLE SOUP

½ pint vegetable puree (see above)
½ oz. margarine or dripping
1 oz. flour
1 pint milk or milk and water

Salt and pepper to taste
2 tablespoons chopped parsley or
    watercress

Melt the margarine or dripping and stir in the flour. Mix until smooth. Add the milk or milk and water and stir until boiling. Boil 5 minutes. Then add the hot vegetable puree just before serving. Mix well and season to taste. Sprinkle with the parsley or watercress just before serving.

QUICK SOUP

2 oz. cabbage
2 oz. onion
4 oz. mixed root vegetables
½ oz. cooking fat or dripping
2 pints of water

1 teaspoon meat extract
2 teaspoons salt
Pinch of pepper
1 tablespoon chopped parsley

Prepare vegetables. Shred the cabbage finely, chop the onion and grate the root vegetables. Melt the fat or dripping and fry the vegetables gently for about 5 minutes. Pour the liquid on to the vegetables, add seasoning and meat extract. Bring to the boil and boil gently for 10-15 minutes; sprinkle with parsley and serve at once.

ONION SOUP AU GRATIN

½ oz. dripping or other fat
4 small onions (½ lb.) thinly sliced
2 pints hot stock (4 beef cubes and
    water)

3 teaspoons salt
¼ teaspoon pepper
4 slices thin toast
4 tablespoons grated cheese

Heat the dripping and fry the sliced onions until soft. Add the hot stock and seasoning, bring to the boil and boil gently for 5-10 minutes. Place the toast at the bottom of the soup plates, sprinkle with grated cheese and pour on the hot soup.

If preferred, grated cheese and dry toast may be handed separately with the soup instead of placing it in the plates.

FISH SOUP

1 lb. fish (haddock if possible)	1 oz. margarine
½ lb. fish trimmings	2 oz. flour
2 pints water	½ pint milk
3 oz. onion or leek	Salt and pepper
2 cloves	1 tablespoon chopped parsley

Wash and clean the fish and trimmings. Place in a pan with the water, onion or leek and cloves. Bring to the boil and skim well. Cook gently for 10 minutes. Lift out the fish. Remove the skin and flake the fish. Cook the stock for half hour longer. Strain the stock and rinse the pan. Melt the margarine, add the flour and cook without colouring, for a few minutes, add the stock and milk and stir until boiling. Add the flaked fish, season and boil gently for 5 minutes. Add the chopped parsley and serve.

SCOTCH BROTH

1 oz. pearl barley	3 oz. onion or leek, sliced
½ lb. boiling beef	2 oz. cabbage, sliced
2 pints water	Salt and pepper
½ lb. carrot, diced	1 tablespoon chopped parsley
1 lb. swede, diced	

Blanch the barley by pouring on boiling water, leaving a minute or two and then straining. Bring barley, beef and water to boil, skim and simmer for 1 hour. Add the prepared vegetables, except the cabbage, salt and pepper and cook for 1½-2 hours longer, add cabbage 15 minutes before serving. Place chopped parsley in the tureen, pour in the broth (after skimming off any superfluous fat). The meat is served as a separate course. Extra vegetables, cut in large pieces may be cooked in the broth to serve round the meat.

VEGETABLE BROTH
WITH SAUSAGE DUMPLINGS

DUMPLINGS

4 oz. self-raising flour
    or 4 oz. plain flour and 2 teaspoons
    baking powder
1 teaspoon salt
1 oz. chopped suet or dripping
1 tablespoon chopped parsley
4 oz. sausage meat
Water to mix

VEGETABLES FOR SOUP

½ lb. carrot
3 oz. turnip
3 oz. onion or leek
4 oz. chopped outer cabbage leaves
½ lb. potatoes
2 pints of stock.

Chop onions or leek, carrots, cabbage, turnip and potatoes, place in the boiling stock and boil gently for half hour. Make dumplings by mixing together all ingredients. If dripping is used it should be rubbed into flour before mixing in other ingredients. Mix with cold water to a fairly stiff consistency and cut into 8 small pieces. Roll into balls and dip in flour. Add to soup, which must be boiling and boil gently for twenty minutes.

How to make SHORT PASTRY

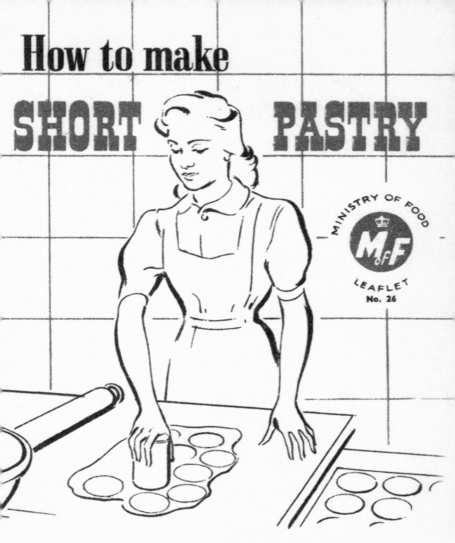

MINISTRY OF FOOD

M of F

LEAFLET
No. 26

Utensils required

A pastry board or any cold smooth surface, such as an enamel topped table or a marble slab; a mixing bowl or basin, wide enough to get both hands in, for rubbing in the fat; a flour sifter or sieve; kitchen knife; rolling-pin; a jug for water and a pair of kitchen scales or a half-pint measure.

All quantities are for 4 persons
All spoon measures are level

INGREDIENTS

8 oz. plain flour (1⅓ level half-pint measures)
½ teaspoon salt
2½-4 oz. fat
Cold water to mix

Lard, cooking fat, clarified dripping and margarine are all suitable fats. Lard and cooking fat make the shortest pastry. Half lard and half margarine is a good mixture for general purposes. A good pastry-maker should not need to use baking-powder, but some cooks find it a help to add 1 level teaspoon of baking-powder if less than 4 oz. fat is being used.

METHOD

1 Weigh or measure the ingredients carefully. If you have no scales measure 1⅓ half-pint level measures for ½ lb. flour.

2 Sift the flour and salt. Sifting adds air to flour and helps to make the pastry lighter. If baking-powder is used sift it with the flour and salt.

3 Rub the fat into the flour using the tips of the fingers, lifting the mixture up and letting it fall into the basin, so mixing in more air. (See illustration.)

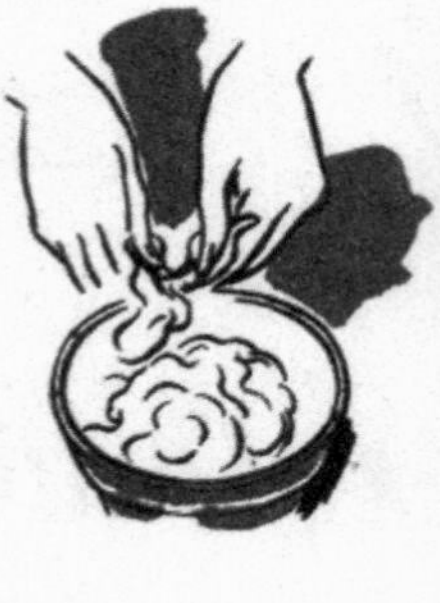

4 Rub until the mixture looks like fine crumbs. This is important if you want a really "short" crust.

5 Add just sufficient water to bind the ingredients and use a knife for mixing. Be careful not to add too much water or the pastry may be tough.

6 Dust the board or table and the rolling-pin with a very little flour and roll the dough lightly. Do not knead the pastry as this tends to make it tough. Handle as little as possible.

The thickness of pastry is largely a matter of personal taste. Some like it thick, others thin, but generally it is best not to have it thicker than ¼ inch or the outside browns before the inside is properly done.

7 Any trimmings left over after cutting the pastry should be gathered together in layers and rolled lightly without kneading. (See illustration.)

8 If the pastry becomes very elastic and springy with too much rolling and handling it is a good plan to put it aside in a cool place for ¼ to ½ hour before baking.

Making a Fruit Pie

Short crust pastry using 6 oz. flour   *2-4 oz. sugar*
2 lb. fruit   *A little water*

1 This is enough for a 2-pint size dish and will give 4-6 helpings. Place a pie funnel or inverted egg cup in the centre of the pie-dish and put the prepared fruit round it. Stone fruit should be picked over and washed; currants should be removed from the stalks; gooseberries topped and tailed; apples peeled, cored and sliced. The fruit should come well up to the top of the pie-dish or the crust will fall in during baking. Add the sugar and a little water. Juicy fruits need less water than others.

2 Cut a strip of pastry the same length and width as the edge of the dish. Moisten the edge and press the strip of pastry round, making a flat join.

3 Roll the main piece of pastry 1 to 2 inches wider than the top of the pie dish. Brush the pastry strip with water and lift the large piece of pastry on top. Ease it on, taking care not to stretch it, and press down the edges.

4 Trim away the surplus pastry (see illustration) and decorate the edge. One way of doing this is to slash the edge with a knife, cutting horizontally. Then with the knife in the right hand use it to scallop the edge of the pie—making the scallops by pressing dents with the thumb of the left hand.

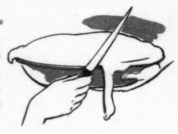

5 Make a slit ½ inch long in the centre top of the pie to allow steam to escape. If a glossy finish is desired brush the top of the pie with beaten egg, or with milk and a sprinkling of sugar.

6 Bake in a hot oven for 35-45 minutes, or until the fruit is cooked. It is a good plan to stand the pie-dish on a shallow baking-tray to catch any juice which bubbles out during cooking.

ALTERNATIVE METHOD FOR COVERING A PIE

Roll the pastry to 1½ inches wider than the top of the pie dish and ease it on. Damp the edge of the dish and fold the overlap of pastry under to make a double edge. Decorate the edge as above.

Making a Fruit Tart

Short pastry using 8 oz. flour   *2-3 oz. sugar*
1½ lb. fruit

This is enough for a 7-8-inch diameter plate or tin and will make 4-6 helpings.

1 Line the dish with pastry, trimming off level with the edge. Use a deep plate or a sandwich-tin.

2 Add fruit and sugar. Prepare fruit as for pie.

3 Place the dish in the centre of another piece of pastry and cut round it leaving a margin of 1-2 inches.

4 Place the pastry on top of the fruit and fold the overhanging top edge under the lower piece of pastry to keep in the juice. (See illustration.) Press edges together.

5 Decorate the edge by pressing the pastry with the first finger of the left hand and pinching the depression with the thumb and first finger of the right hand. (See illustration.)

6 The top may be glazed or not, as desired. Cut a slit ½-inch long in the centre top.

7 Bake in a hot oven for 40-50 minutes, or until the fruit is tender.

Making a Flan Case

1 Roll the pastry 1 to 2 inches larger than the flan ring or sandwich-tin. If a flan ring is used it should be stood on a baking-tray.

2 Fit the pastry into the ring, or tin, pressing it firmly against the bottom and sides.

3 Remove surplus pastry by rolling over the top with a rolling-pin. The edge may be left plain or decorated.

4 Put a few crusts of bread in the bottom of the flan to prevent it rising.

5 Bake in a very hot oven for 10-15 minutes.

6 Remove crusts and take the case out of the ring or tin. Fill with any desired filling, sweet or savoury.

Making Jam Tarts

1 Use a cup, tin or pastry cutter and cut pastry with a sharp tap, this makes a clean cut and the edges of the pastry will rise well.

2 Place the rounds in the patty tins.

3 Add a little jam to each. Do not fill too full or the jam will bubble over during cooking.

4 Bake in a hot oven for 10-15 minutes.

Making Turnovers

1 Roll pastry and cut in large circles using an inverted saucer as a guide.

2 Place a little filling in one half, moisten the edges and fold pastry in half.

3 Press the edges together and decorate. Cut a slit ½-inch long in the top and brush with egg or milk.

4 Bake in a hot oven for 15-20 minutes.

Making a lattice top Treacle Tart

Short pastry using 8 oz. flour
6 level tablespoons breadcrumbs
6 level tablespoons golden syrup

Lemon juice or lemon substitute
½ level teaspoon ground ginger

1 Line a plate with pastry.

2 Mix the crumbs, syrup and flavourings, spread in the pastry case. Moisten the edge of the pastry.

3 Cut thin strips of pastry and cover the top with a criss-cross of these, twisting each strip. (See illustration.)

4 Brush edges again and cover with a strip of pastry the width of the edge. This covers up the ends of the lattice. (See illustration.)

5 Press edge with a fork.

6 Bake in a hot oven for 20-30 minutes.

Making Cornish Pasties

Short pastry using 8 oz. flour
8 oz. raw minced beef
4 oz. cooked mashed or raw, grated or diced potato

1 onion chopped finely
2 tablespoons chopped parsley
Salt and pepper

1 Roll the pastry and cut in large rounds using a saucer or small plate as a guide.

2 Mix the filling and place some in the centre of each round.

3 Moisten the edges of the pastry and press them together on top of the filling, making an upstanding edge.

4 Pinch the edge into scallops.

5 Prick the sides of the pasties and brush with egg or milk.

6 Bake in a hot oven for 30-40 minutes.

TART & PIE FILLINGS

Each enough for 8 oz. pastry.

Apple Filling

2 oz. prunes
4 oz. apple rings or
½ lb. fresh apples
2 oz. dates

2 oz. sultanas
2 level tablespoons syrup
4 oz. bread crumbs
1 level teaspoon mixed spice

Soak the prunes overnight with the apple rings, if these are used instead of fresh apples. Chop the prunes, apple rings or apples, and dates and mix thoroughly with the other ingredients. Line a fireproof plate, 8 inch in diameter, with half of the pastry, spread with the filling and cover with the remaining pastry. Sprinkle sugar lightly on top and bake in a hot oven for 30-40 minutes.

Jam Filling

2 level tablespoons jam
(Blackcurrant if possible)

4 tablespoons boiling water
8 level tablespoons breadcrumbs

Mix the jam with the water and stir in the breadcrumbs. Line a 7½-inch sandwich tin with pastry and add the jam filling. Bake in a hot oven for 20-30 minutes. Serve hot or cold.

Prune Filling

8 oz. prunes

1 pint water

4 level tablespoons sugar

3 level tablespoons flour

1½ tablespoons lemon squash

Cook the prunes in the water, strain, stone and cut up. Mix with the other ingredients. Line a 6-inch flan or sandwich tin with pastry, add the prune filling, cover with pastry and bake in a hot oven for 30-40 minutes.

The liquor from the cooked prunes should be kept and used for making a sweet sauce or as a cold drink.

Cheese & Vegetable Filling

¾ lb. mixed cooked vegetables (including cooked dried peas, beans, or lentils)

2 level tablespoons grated cheese

1 tablespoon parsley, coarsley chopped

Salt, pepper and mustard

¼ pint white sauce

Mix the ingredients together and turn into a pastry lined 7-inch flan or sandwich tin, cover with pastry, brush the top with egg or milk and sprinkle with a little grated cheese. Bake in a moderately hot oven for 20-30 minutes. Serve hot with vegetables or cold with salad.

Pilchard Filling

1 small tin pilchards (12 oz.)

2 tablespoons parsley

2 level tablespoons chopped onion

2 oz. mashed potato

1 level teaspoon salt

½ level teaspoon pepper

Mash the fish and mix with the other ingredients. Line a 7-inch sandwich tin with pastry, add the filling and cover with pastry. Bake in a hot oven for ½ hour.

NOTE.—Some of the recipes given in this leaflet are demonstrated in the film, "How to Make Short Pastry", made by the Central Office of Information for the Ministry of Food and the Ministry of Education.

8

Issued by the Ministry of Food
Reprinted January, 1947

Ppt. Ltd.   6493603

FRUIT BOTTLING
including Tomatoes

Important Points to Remember

1

CHOOSING JARS

Although there are many kinds of preserving jars, the principle behind each is the same. The jar is closed with a glass or metal lid which rests on a rubber ring to make the joint airtight. While the contents of the jar are cooling, the lid is held tightly in place by a screwband, a spring clip, a weight, a second metal lid or some other mechanical grip. When the jar is cold, the lid is sealed in position by the vacuum formed inside. The jar is now airtight and no longer depends on the tightness of the screwband or grip to hold down the lid.

Before buying preserving jars, make sure that there are no chips or ridges, etc., on the mouth which might prevent the lid and rubber ring from fitting properly. You can make sure a jam jar has an even mouth, after testing for ridges, by inverting it on a perfectly level surface, when it should stand firmly and not rock. If you use the special lids sold to fit on jam jars, choose jars that have smooth and quite circular mouths and make certain that the lids fit properly.

When buying rubber rings, take a sample jar or ring with you to get the right size. Be sure to buy good quality rings; they feel elastic and will spring back after slight stretching.

2

TESTING JARS BEFORE USE

Fill the jar with water and put on the rubber ring, lid and screwband or other grip. Then wipe the outside of the jar and stand it upside down for half an hour (see top of page 2). If any water leaks out, examine the jar for defects. A different rubber ring may remedy the fault. With the clip type of seal, you

1

may find it necessary either to bend the clip so that it grips more tightly, or to use a new clip. A penny pushed under the centre of the clip often makes a tighter fit.

3 PREPARING THE FRUIT

Fruit for bottling should be just fully ripe, except gooseberries which are best when green and hard. It is a waste of time and money to bottle bruised or over-ripe fruit so look over the fruit very thoroughly and discard any which is not in good condition.

- **Soft Fruit.** Pick over carefully and rinse in cold water. If gooseberries are to be bottled in syrup, they need a small slice cut off when "topping and tailing" to prevent shrivelling.
- **Stone Fruit.** Remove any stems and rinse in cold water. Large fruit can be stoned and packed in halves. Peaches dipped in boiling water for a few seconds can be peeled easily.
- **Hard Fruit.** Apples will not brown so readily if you put them in salt water (1 level tablespoon salt to 1 quart water) as soon as they are peeled. Drain, rinse and then plunge them into boiling water for two or three minutes to soften them slightly so that they will pack more easily. Pears should be put in salt water, like apples, to prevent browning, and packed and processed as quickly as possible afterwards.
  Cooking pears or quinces should be stewed until tender.
- **Tomatoes.** Wash thoroughly and preserve with or without skins. These can easily be peeled off if the tomatoes are put into boiling water for 10 to 15 seconds and then dipped in cold water.
- **Tomatoes in their own Juice.** Skin and cut medium or large ones into halves or quarters. Pack tightly in the jars, sprinkling salt on each layer—1 level tablespoon to every 2 lb. tomatoes. A teaspoon of sugar added to each jar will improve the flavour. Press the tomatoes well down in the jars. Do not add any liquid.

4 PROCESSING

No method of bottling will be successful unless the fruit is heated properly and the seal on every bottle is airtight. Therefore follow the directions carefully and make sure the correct temperatures and times are reached during processing; this is particularly important when using Method 3.

5 TO TEST THE SEAL AFTER BOTTLING

The day after bottling remove the screwbands or other grips and lift each jar by its lid. Every jar that can be lifted in this way has a perfect seal. If the lid comes off, the fruit must be eaten within a few days, or if you wish to re-seal, look for the fault which led to the failure to form a vacuum, and having put this right, re-process the fruit and seal again.
Note: Remember that even a perfect seal is no guarantee that the fruit will keep unless the process has been done correctly.

6 SYRUP FOR BOTTLING

Sugar syrup or water can be used for any of the methods described. If a sugar syrup is used the flavour is better and the fruit is ready for use when the bottles are opened.

Use from 4 to 8 oz. sugar to a pint of water according to the kind of fruit and the degree of sweetness required. Dissolve the sugar and allow the syrup to boil for a few minutes. Use this hot or cold according to the directions in the method chosen.

BRINE FOR TOMATOES

To each two pints of water, add one level tablespoon of salt, and, if required, ¼ oz. sugar to improve the flavour. Bring the salt, sugar and water to the boil and use as directed.

METHOD 1

WATER BATH METHOD

For this method you need a pan deep enough to allow the jars to be completely covered with water. A sterilizer, zinc bath, large fish kettle, or even a clean bucket will do. It must be arranged so that the jars do not touch the bottom or sides of the pan. A false bottom can be made by nailing together strips of wood in trellis fashion, or a folded cloth can be used. If no lid is available, use a pastry board.

Wash and drain the jars and lids. Put the rubber rings to soak in warm water, and dip in boiling water just before use.

Pack the fruit tightly almost to the top of the jars. Shake soft juicy fruits down; the handle of a wooden spoon is useful for packing hard fruits tightly in layers.

Fill the jars to overflowing with cold water or syrup. Tomatoes should be covered with cold brine.

Put the rubber rings and lids in position and fasten with the screwbands or other grips. Screwbands should be tightened up and THEN UNSCREWED A QUARTER TURN TO ALLOW FOR EXPANSION.

Stand the jars in the pan so that they do not touch one another or the sides of the pan. Cover the jars completely with cold water. Put on the lid, and heat slowly. For times and temperatures see "Processing Chart."

Take out enough water with a cup or jug to uncover the shoulders of the jars. Holding them by the shoulder, lift one jar at a time out of the pan, stand it on a wooden table or board and tighten the screwband or see that the clip or other grip is holding properly. Put the jars aside to cool.

Note: Do not take out several jars of the screwband type at once. Each jar must be screwed up with the least possible delay while it is still hot. As the jars cool, the screwbands need further tightening up.

METHOD 2

OVEN METHOD (Heating without Liquid)

Wash and drain the jars, there is no need to dry them. Pack the fruit tightly into the jars, right to the top, as the fruit shrinks during cooking.

Put the jars in a very moderate oven (about 240°F.), covering with a tin to prevent discolouring. The jars must be placed on an asbestos mat, piece of cardboard or wood, so that they do not touch the oven shelf. Process according to time on "Processing Chart" overleaf.

Put the rubber rings and lids in a pan of water and bring to the boil to sterilize them. They must be hot when placed on the jars. If using metal lids which are difficult to handle when hot, fit on the rubber rings before heating the lids. Screwbands and clips need not be heated. Remove the jars one at a time from

the oven and fill to overflowing with boiling water or syrup. If the fruit has shrunk very much, quickly fill up with fruit from an extra bottle heated with the others, before adding the boiling liquid. Put the rubber ring and lid on at once and fasten down with screwband or other grip. Each jar must be sealed before the next jar is taken out of the oven. As the sealed jars cool, screwbands may need tightening.

After cooling for 24 hours, test and store as described on pages 2 and 5.

Note: This method is not as satisfactory for apples, pears, quinces or tomatoes as the "Water Bath" method.

METHOD 3

OVEN METHOD (Heating with Liquid)

This method is similar to method 2, but the jars are filled with liquid, either sugar syrup, brine or water, before processing in the oven.

Pack the fruit into the jars as in Method 1 and fill *to within ¼ inch of the top* with cold liquid.

Put the rubber rings and lids in position and fasten with spring grips. If using screwbands, these should not be put on until after processing.

Put the jars in a baking tin with about 1 inch depth of warm water. Then place in an oven at 300°F. (about the same temperature as for a rich fruit cake) and keep at that temperature for the times given in the "Processing Chart" (see page 6).

Remove the jars, one at a time from the oven, with a dry cloth and stand on a wooden board or table away from the draught. If using screwbands, fasten the jars with these immediately; they may need further tightening as the jars cool.

Let the jars cool for 24 hours, then test the seal as described on page 2.

Note: Jars with wire bailed caps should not be used for this method.

METHOD 4

PULPING

This is a simple way of bottling either hard or soft stewed fruit. It can be used for windfall apples or bruised plums if all the bruised parts are first removed, and for tomatoes.

A deep pan is needed as described in "Water Bath" method.

Wash, drain and heat the jars and lids. Put the rubber rings in a pan of water and bring to the boil just before they are put on the jars.

Stew the fruit in a little water until thoroughly pulped, using only enough water to prevent burning.

Tomatoes can be skinned before pulping, or cut up, cooked with seasonings and then rubbed through a sieve to remove the skins and seeds.

Damsons may be cooked whole, and apples without peeling or coring, if they are sieved in the same way. Remember though, that the pulp in all cases must be put back in the pan and brought to the boil again before bottling.

When the fruit is thoroughly pulped, pour at once into the hot jars. Seal immediately with rubber ring, lid and screwband or other grip. Tighten the screwband and THEN UNSCREW A QUARTER TURN TO ALLOW FOR EXPANSION.

Put the jars in BOILING water in a deep pan as described in "Water Bath" Method and boil for time given for pulping on "Processing Chart." The jars must be completely covered by the water.

Remove the jars, one at a time, and tighten the screwbands or see that the clips or other grips are properly in position. As the jars cool, screwbands may need tightening.

After cooling for 24 hours test as described on page 2.

STORAGE

The filled jars should be stored in a cool, dark place; light destroys the colour of the fruit. A label with the date will show which jar should be used first. The screwbands, clips or other grips should be removed and greased to prevent rusting. They should be stored in a dry place until wanted again. Screwbands can be replaced on the jars but should not be screwed down tightly.

To open the bottles, insert the point of a knife on the rubber ring and very gently lever upwards until a stream of air enters. It will be easier to remove the lids if the jars are stood in hot water for a few minutes.

Note: **Vegetables must not be bottled by any of these methods.**

5

PROCESSING CHART FOR BOTTLING FRUIT

FRUIT GROUP	WATER BATH METHOD 1		OVEN METHOD 2 — Heating without liquid	OVEN METHOD 3 — Heating with liquid	PULPING METHOD 4
	With thermometer *Temperature reached in 1¼ hours*	Without thermometer *Temperature reached in 1 hour*	Oven heat—slow	Oven heat—very moderate	Jars placed in hot water and brought to the boil
1 Apples (in syrup) Apricots Blackberries Damsons Gooseberries Greengages Loganberries Raspberries Rhubarb Strawberries	165°F. Maintain for a further 10 minutes	Simmering Maintain for a further 5 minutes	240°F. ½–1 hour	300–320°F. 1¼ hours	Boil for 5 minutes
2 Apples (solid pack) Cherries Currants (black, red, white) Grapes Peaches Plums	180°F. Maintain for a further 15 minutes	Simmering Maintain for a further 15 minutes	240°F. 1–1¼ hours	300–320°F. 80 minutes	Boil for 5 minutes
3 Pears Quinces Tomatoes	190°F. Maintain for a further 30 minutes	Simmering Maintain for a further 30 minutes	At least 1¼ hours. Safer processed by Methods 1 or 3	300–320°F. 95 minutes	Boil for 10 minutes

THE ABC OF PRESERVING is a 40-page handbook that describes the best ways of making jams, marmalades, jellies and syrups; bottling, canning and drying fruit and vegetables; making pickles, chutneys and sauces. Over 70 recipes and 40 illustrations.
Price 6d. from or through any bookseller or by post 8d. from H.M. Stationery Office, P.O. Box 569, London, S.E.1.

JOINT LEAFLET ISSUED BY THE MINISTRY OF FOOD AND THE MINISTRY OF AGRICULTURE AND FISHERIES

GREEN VEGETABLES

No country in the world grows vegetables better than we do, and probably no country in the world cooks them worse. For generations we have wasted our root vegetables by excessive peeling and over-cooking, and boiled most of the goodness out of our green vegetables—only to pour it down the sink.

When fresh fruit is short we need green vegetables more than ever because they all contain the important fresh fruit vitamin, Vitamin C. Some have more than others. Brussels Sprouts, parsley and watercress all contain more than oranges; cabbage, cauliflower, spinach, swedes, broccoli, turnip tops and kale are all good sources of this vitamin. Not only do green vegetables give us vitamin C, but also vitamins A and B, iron and calcium. Green peas and beans, broad, French and runner, make a welcome change in the menu, but remember they do not take the place of the leafy, green vegetables, as they contain only a little vitamin C. See that you have a salad a day as well as peas and beans when they are in season.

MINISTRY OF FOOD

MF of

LEAFLET

No. 1

GREEN VEGETABLES should be served in other ways than as an accompaniment to a meat course. They make excellent supper or lunch dishes, combined with cheese, eggs, bacon, meat or milk. They are invaluable raw as sandwich fillings and also as salad served with hot or cold dishes.

For healthy eating plan to have a green leafy vegetable at least once every day.

If vegetables are cooked carelessly much of their food value is lost. Their vitamin C—the fresh fruit vitamin—is easily destroyed by bad cooking. Throwing away the cooking water also wastes valuable mineral salts and vitamins.

So when you cook green vegetables follow these rules:

GENERAL RULES FOR ALL
GREEN VEGETABLES

1 Use as fresh as possible. If you grow your own vegetables do not gather until you actually need them.

2 Wash the vegetables thoroughly, but avoid soaking where possible and never soak for long. Half an hour in cold salted water is enough for even the most tight-hearted cabbage.

3 Never drown vegetables. You need only just enough water to keep the pan from burning. Allow $\frac{1}{4}$ pint of water and 1 dessertspoon of salt for each 2 lb. of vegetables. The water must be boiling before the vegetables are added.

4 Cook with the lid on the pan. If you have no lid a plate can be used. This point is important because the vegetables are to be "steam-boiled" and if the steam is allowed to escape the pan will go dry and burn.

5 Boil briskly for 10-15 minutes, giving the pan an occasional shake.

6 Drain off any liquid and use for making soups and gravies or thicken with flour and use as a sauce. See recipe.

7 Serve the vegetables at once. Keeping hot or re-heating will destroy the vitamin C. Before serving, if you can spare it, add a teaspoonful of margarine to the vegetables and toss them well.

If these suggestions are followed the vegetables will be crisp and full of flavour. They will also retain the greater part of their vitamin and mineral salts.

CABBAGE, SAVOY & RED CABBAGE

Allow 1½ lb. for 4 portions. Remove the dark or coarse outer leaves and use them shredded in soups or stews. Do not throw them away because they contain more of the vitamins and mineral salts than the more tender inner leaves. Cut the cabbage in quarters and wash well. Then shred with a sharp knife cutting across from top to stem. Cook quickly in a little water as described in General Rules. All sorts of additions may be made to cabbage or savoys cooked in this way. A few bacon rinds chopped small; a few teaspoons of vinegar and a sprinkling of nutmeg, or perhaps a shake of caraway seeds, and you have something quite new and intriguing.

SPRING GREENS

Allow 1½ lb. for 4 portions. Wash well and shred with a sharp knife. Treat in the same way as cabbage.

KALE

Allow 2 lb. for 4 portions. Wash well and unless the kale is very young and tender strip the leaves off the tougher stalks. Use the stalks for soup or stock. If the leaves are large shred them before cooking in the same way as cabbage.

SPINACH

Allow 2 lb. for 4 portions. Wash the spinach very thoroughly, shake and put in a pan without any water. Sprinkle with a little salt, put on the lid and cook gently until tender (about 10 minutes). Drain and serve or if preferred, the spinach may be chopped and a little margarine and pepper added, with a pinch of mace or nutmeg.

TOPS

Allow 1½ lb. for 4 portions. Broccoli tops, turnip tops and beetroot tops have good food value and are excellent if cooked as already described for cabbage. So are the broad bean tops which gardeners always pick off.

BRUSSELS SPROUTS

Allow 1½ lb. for 4 portions. Remove any decayed leaves and wash well. Cut very large sprouts in half. Cook as described in "General Rules for all Green Vegetables."

CAULIFLOWER & BROCCOLI

Allow 1 large head for 4 portions. Break into sprigs and wash well. Cook as described in "General Rules for all Green Vegetables." When buying cauliflowers, always ask for the leaves as well as the flower, as the leaves make a dish by themselves if cooked as cabbage. The stalks, cooked until tender in a very little boiling salted water and then drained, rolled in brown breadcrumbs and quickly fried in a very little hot fat or browned in the oven, have a nutty flavour and are a new dish to most people. They are also delicious grated raw in a salad. If peeled, the whole stem, from the root up, can be used.

SEAKALE BEET, SWISS CHARD OR SILVER BEET

Allow 1½ lb. for 4 portions. The green leaves may be cooked separately as spinach and the white stalks cooked and served in the same way as celery, which it resembles in texture though not in flavour. When it is to be served as an accompaniment to meat and potatoes, the best flavour is obtained by cooking the leaves and stalks together. Slice the stalks and boil with the green tops in the same way as cabbage. Drain, season well with pepper, nutmeg or mace, and if possible, add a little fat.

YOUNG NETTLES

Allow 2 lb. for 4 portions. Pick only the very young and tender leaves, using gloves for picking. Wash well, cook and serve in the same way as cabbage.

PEAS

Allow 2 lb. for 4 portions, but the amount depends on the fullness of the pods. When boiling fresh garden peas put a teaspoonful of sugar, if possible, and a little salt in the water as well as the mint, and be careful not to cook them too long or too fast, or they will come out of their skins. If you are cooking another vegetable, peas are delicious cooked in a steamer on the top. Sprinkle with a pinch of salt and put a sprig of mint with them in the steamer. Save the water for soup and gravy.

FRENCH OR RUNNER BEANS

Allow 1½ lb. for 4 portions. When young, cook whole with only the tops and tails removed. When older, the stringy vein which develops along the rib of the pod must be removed. Most housewives like to slice the beans lengthwise, but it is a great saving in time to break them with the fingers into 2 inch lengths, and less flavour is lost this way. Boil until tender in a very small amount of salted water. If you like your beans to glisten, add a teaspoonful of fat to the water. Be sure to save the water. It is good as a drink by itself or for gravy or soup.

BROAD BEANS

Allow 2-4 lb. for 4 portions. The amount needed depends on the fullness of the pods. When young, broad beans can be cooked, unshelled, in a little boiling salted water and eaten pod and all. Or the beans can be shelled and the pods sliced. The cooked sliced pods are very good as a hot vegetable or served cold in salad. When the beans are older the pods are too tough to eat as a vegetable, but make good stock for soup. Broad beans which have been allowed to mature in their pods may be stored for winter use. Make sure they are quite dry before packing in airtight tins. Soak and use as haricots.

RECIPES

SAUCE FOR VEGETABLES

½ oz. margarine, fat or dripping   ½ pint hot vegetable stock
2 tablespoons flour   Salt and pepper
Pinch of nutmeg (optional)

Cook the vegetables as described under "General Rules for all Green Vegetables," strain and keep the vegetable water, making it up to half a pint if necessary with hot water. Melt the fat in the saucepan and mix in the flour, stirring until it is well blended. Add the vegetable water and stir until the mixture boils. Boil 5 minutes. Add seasoning (salt may not be needed as there will be some in the vegetable stock), nutmeg, if used, and the vegetables. Mix well and serve at once.

CREAMED CABBAGE

¾ pint water   ½ oz. margarine or dripping
1½ lb. shredded cabbage   3 tablespoons flour
2 teaspoons salt   4 tablespoons grated cheese
Pinch of pepper

Boil half a pint of water, add the cabbage and salt and boil 5 minutes. Add the margarine to this. Blend the flour and cheese with the remaining ¼ pint of water, add to the cabbage, season well and cook for another 10 minutes. Serve hot. Suitable for a lunch or supper dish.

PIQUANTE SPINACH

3 lb. spinach   2 teaspoons salt
1½ rashers bacon   3 teaspoons horseradish sauce

Wash and prepare the spinach. Chop bacon and fry till golden brown. Add spinach and salt and moisten with a very little water. Cook until tender. Strain and chop well. Mix in horseradish and serve at once.

BEANS BEARNAISE

1 lb. runner beans   2 tomatoes, chopped
Small knob of fat   Salt and pepper
1 oz. bacon chopped

Break beans into short lengths and cook until tender in a very little boiling salted water. Drain and keep hot. Place fat in pan and fry bacon and tomatoes. When cooked add the beans and mix well. Season and serve.

BROCCOLI or CAULIFLOWER with HOLLANDAISE SAUCE

1 large or 2 small broccoli or cauliflowers
2 tablespoons flour
½ pint milk or stock, or vegetable water

4 peppercorns (in muslin bag)
2 dried eggs, reconstituted
3 tablespoons vinegar
Pepper and salt

Separate broccoli or cauliflower into small pieces and boil until tender in. very little salted water. Drain. Mix the flour to a smooth paste with a little of the milk or stock, boil remainder, pour on to flour, return to pan, stir until it boils, and boil 5 minutes with the peppercorns. Remove from heat and add the eggs carefully, boil 2-3 minutes longer. Remove the peppercorns, add vinegar and seasoning and pour over the broccoli or cauliflower.

BRUSSELS SPROUTS A L'ITALIENNE

1 lb. Brussels sprouts
Salt
1 oz. margarine
1 oz. flour
1 pint milk and vegetable water

Salt and pepper
Pinch of grated nutmeg
Lemon substitute
2-3 oz. grated cheese

Wash and clean the sprouts; cook in a little boiling salted water until tender. Drain, keeping the vegetable water. Melt the fat, add the flour and cook for about 2 minutes. Add the liquid, bring to the boil and cook for 5 minutes. Add seasoning to taste, grated nutmeg, a few drops of lemon substitute and grated cheese. Mix thoroughly. Add the sprouts to the sauce and heat through. Serve hot.

RED CABBAGE

1 oz. fat or dripping
1 lb. red cabbage, shredded
1 large onion, sliced
1 large apple, sliced
2 tablespoons stock or water

1 tablespoon vinegar
Salt and pepper
2 teaspoons of sugar, brown if possible

Melt the fat in a saucepan and add all the other ingredients. Cover with a tightly fitting lid and boil gently until the cabbage is tender, about 30-40 minutes. Shake the pan occasionally during cooking to prevent the cabbage from sticking. Do not cook over a fierce heat or the cabbage will boil dry. This is excellent served with pork or with grilled or fried sausages.

Ask for Ministry of Food Leaflet "Salads" and "Root Vegetables" or send a postcard to:

Food Advice Service, Ministry of Food, London W.1.

The Ministry of Food has compiled the "ABC of Cookery" which gives suggestions and methods for cooking and preparing food. Obtainable from H.M. Stationery Office or through any Bookseller. Price 1/- or 1/2 by post.

Issued by the Ministry of Food

Ppt. Ltd. 51-2000

6492301

January, 1946

MAKING THE MOST
OF THE
Fat Ration

TRY THESE FAT SAVING HINTS AND RECIPES.

FAT FOR SPREADING

Butter Extender No. 1

8 oz. margarine or butter   ½ level teaspoon salt
1 level tablespoon flour   ½ pint milk

Put 6 oz. margarine into a bowl and cream with a wooden spoon. Melt 2 oz. in a saucepan, work in the flour and salt and add the milk. Heat carefully, stirring until smooth and thick. Boil 5-7 minutes. Cool and add to the margarine in the bowl. Mix well until smooth and allow to cool before using.

Butter Extender No. 2

Melt margarine and add it to an equal quantity of mashed potato. Mix and use cold.

Dripping Spreads

Use dripping from the joint alone, or mixed with any of the following: Salt and pepper, chopped pickle, meat extract, chopped onion or leek, bottle sauce or chutney, herbs, vinegar and grated cheese.

COLLECTING EXTRA FAT

Trim all surplus fat off cooked or uncooked meat and render it down. Firm fat may be grated or chopped finely and used instead of suet.

Bacon Rinds

Bake or fry these until crisp and all the fat has been extracted. Strain off the fat and use in place of dripping. The crisp rinds may be chopped and used for flavouring scrambled eggs, sandwich spreads, soups, stews or stock.

To Render Down Fat (Method 1)

Cut the fat in small pieces and put into a pan. Add sufficient water to cover the bottom of the saucepan and bring to the boil. Skim well. Boil gently on a low heat, stirring occasionally to prevent the fat from sticking. Continue cooking gently until all the water has evaporated and the pieces look dried up and sink to the bottom. Allow the fat to cool slightly and then strain, pressing the pieces of tissue against the sides of the strainer.

To Render Down Fat *(Method 2)*

Cut the fat in small pieces and place in a pan in a slow oven until the fat has melted, and there are only crisp brown pieces of tissue left. Strain into a clean basin, pressing the pieces of tissue against the sides of the strainer.

NOTE.—In both cases take care not to have the heat too fierce or the fat will burn and be spoiled. The small brown pieces of tissue left after the fat has been extracted should not be wasted. They are excellent used in savoury pies, stews, mixed with meat in rissoles, cottage pie, etc.

CLEANING USED FAT

Save all fat from the tops of stews, soups, gravy, etc., and the dripping from roasting, frying, and grilling. This fat needs to be clarified, or cleaned before it is used for cakes, pastry or frying, but may be used as it is for savoury pastry and sandwich spreads.

To clarify Fat

Put the fat in a saucepan and cover with water. Bring slowly to the boil, pour into a bowl and leave to get cold. Remove the fat from the top of the water, scrape the bottom of it and heat in a saucepan slowly to drive off any remaining water.

When the fat ceases to bubble it means all the water has been evaporated. If water is left in, the fat will not keep, and it will "splutter" badly when used for frying.

USES FOR CLARIFIED FAT

1. Use for frying any type of food.
2. Use in pastry either in place of margarine and cooking fats, or mixed with them. Fat flavoured with onion, etc., should only be used for pastry for savoury pies and tarts.
3. Use in cakes, buns and biscuits, in place of margarine, and cooking fat or mixed with them. Fat flavoured with onion should not be used.

SAVING FAT WHEN FRYING

1. Be careful not to let frying fat burn. Strain carefully after use. The same fat can be used many times.
2. Use moisture free fat. Water in fat makes it splutter all over the stove and is wasteful and dirty. (To remove water see second step in clarifying fat).
3. For fried potatoes, boil first and then slice and brown in a little fat.
4. Fry herrings and sprats without any fat in the pan. Warm the pan and sprinkle with salt before adding the fish. These fish are good grilled and no fat need be added.
5. Bake or grill rissoles and fish cakes instead of frying.

USING WRAPPING PAPERS

Always scrape the butter, margarine and cooking fat papers with a knife so as not to waste a scrap. Save the paper to use for greasing cake tins and pudding basins and for covers for steamed puddings and dishes baked in the oven. They are also useful for wrapping round cheese to keep it fresh.

MAIN DISHES

Oven Fried Fish (serves four)

1 level tablespoon flour	2 tablespoons milk
½ level teaspoon salt	1-1½ lb. fillet of fish, cut in
Pinch of pepper	pieces
Pinch of grated nutmeg	Browned breadcrumbs

Blend the flour, salt, pepper and nutmeg with the milk. Dip the pieces of fish in this and then roll in browned crumbs. Arrange the fish in a well-greased pie dish and cover with greased paper. Bake in a hot oven for 30 minutes.

NOTE.—The pieces of fish can be sprinkled with salt and pepper and coated in breadcrumbs only. If it can be spared, up to 1 oz. cooking fat or dripping can be heated in the pie dish before adding the fish.

Meat Cakes without Fat (serves four)

4 oz. mashed potato	1 medium onion, chopped
4 oz. corned beef or	finely
chopped cooked meat	1 teaspoon brown sauce
2 tablespoons gravy	Pinch of pepper and salt

Mix the ingredients thoroughly together. Put in four heaps on a greased baking tray, cover with paper or another tray, and bake in a moderate oven for 10-15 minutes. Serve hot with gravy and vegetables, or cold with salad.

Baked Mutton Mould (serves four)

1-2 level tablespoons browned	½-1 level teaspoon mixed herbs
breadcrumbs	1-2 level teaspoons salt
8 oz. cold cooked mutton,	½ level teaspoon pepper
finely minced	1 egg, fresh or dried
2 oz. onion, finely minced	1 tablespoon tomato sauce
2 oz. fresh breadcrumbs	2 tablespoons water or stock

Grease a 1 lb. cake tin and coat the inside with the browned breadcrumbs. Mix all the ingredients together very well. Turn the mixture into the tin and bake in a moderate oven for 45 minutes. Turn out and **serve** hot with vegetables and gravy, or cold with a salad.

Roast Potatoes

Roasting potatoes round the joint uses more fat than if the potatoes are cooked separately as follows:—

METHOD 1

Slice potatoes and place in a greased tin and they will brown without any added fat.

METHOD 2

2 lb. potatoes	1 level dessertspoon salt
1 pint water	

Peel the potatoes thinly and put into a roasting tin with the water, and salt. There should be enough room for them to lie comfortably without touching and there should be enough water to half fill the roasting tin. Put the tin into a hot oven and bake for 1½ hours. The water evaporates and leaves shiny golden balls with floury insides.

PUDDINGS

Steamed Chocolate or Ginger Pudding
(serves four)

6 oz. plain flour

4 level teaspoons baking
powder

¼ level teaspoon salt

2 level tablespoons cocoa or

1½-2 level teaspoons ground
ginger

2 oz. sugar

1 egg, fresh or dried

About ¼ pint milk and water
to mix

Sift all the dry ingredients together and beat to a thick batter with
the egg and milk and water. Pour into a greased 1½ pint basin, cover
and steam for 1¼-1½ hours.

Mock Suet Pudding with Jam or Syrup
(serves four)

8 oz. plain flour and

4 level teaspoons baking
powder or

8 oz. self-raising flour

1 level tablespoon dried egg,
dry (optional)

½ level teaspoon salt

About ¼ pint milk and water
to mix

4 level tablespoons jam or
syrup

Mix all the dry ingredients together and add enough liquid to make a
dropping consistency. Grease a 1½ pint basin and place the jam or syrup
at the bottom. Drop the pudding mixture on top, cover with a greased
paper and steam for 1-1½ hours. Serve with jam or syrup sauce, or
custard.

Mock Suet Pudding with Fruit (serves four)

Omit the jam or syrup and add 2 oz. sugar and 2 oz. dried fruit with
the flour.

Bread and Marmalade Pudding (serves four)

4 oz. breadcrumbs
1 pint milk

3-4 level tablespoons
marmalade

Place half the breadcrumbs in a pie-dish and spread with the
marmalade. Cover with the remaining crumbs and add the milk. Bake
in a moderately hot oven for 1-1½ hours, when the pudding should be
set and golden brown.

Orange or Lemon Whip (serves four)

4 level tablespoons cornflour
or 8 level tablespoons flour

1-2 level tablespoons sugar

6 tablespoons orange or lemon
squash made up to 1 pint
with water

Mix the dry ingredients to a smooth paste with a little of the liquid.
Bring the remainder to the boil and pour on to the blended mixture.
Return to the pan, bring to the boil, and boil gently for five minutes,
stirring frequently. Leave to cool, then whisk until light and frothy. Serve
in individual glasses.
N.B.—4-6 level tablespoons custard powder may be used in place of
the cornflour.

Milk Jelly Whip (serves four)

A 1 pint packet of jelly, or
jelly crystals

¼ pint evaporated milk
Colouring if necessary

Dissolve the jelly, following the directions given on the packet, but
making it up to ¾ pint instead of 1 pint. Leave to cool and when just
beginning to set, stir in the evaporated milk and colouring if necessary;
whisk till light and frothy. Serve cold in a bowl or in individual glasses.

Baked Fruit Pie (serves four)

2 lb. fruit, bottled or fresh
4 oz. stale bread

3 tablespoons milk or water
2 level tablespoons sugar

If fresh fruit is used, stew first and sweeten to taste. Put the fruit and juice in a pie dish. Cut the bread neatly into small cubes and place on top of the fruit. Pour the milk over the bread and sprinkle on the sugar. Bake in a hot oven 20-30 minutes.

CAKES AND PASTRY

Gingerbread without Fat (serves four)

4 oz. plain flour
3 oz. medium oatmeal
2 level teaspoons ground
ginger
2 level teaspoons mixed spice

2 oz. sugar
¼ pint milk
3 level tablespoons treacle or
syrup
1 level teaspoon bicarbonate
of soda

Mix the flour, oatmeal, ginger, spice and sugar in a basin. Heat the milk and treacle or syrup in a pan and bring to the boil. Add the soda and stir until dissolved. Pour into the dry ingredients and mix quickly and thoroughly. Turn into a well greased shallow tin, about 9 inches by 6 inches, and bake in a moderate oven for about 50 minutes.

Dripping Cake (serves four)

8 oz. self-raising flour or
8 oz. plain flour and
4 level teaspoons baking
powder
½ level teaspoon salt

¼ level teaspoon mixed spice
2 oz. clarified dripping
3 oz. sugar
3 oz. any dried fruit
¼ pint milk

Sift the flour, baking powder if used, salt and spices together. Rub in the fat and add the sugar and fruit. Mix to a soft consistency with the milk and turn into a greased 6 inch cake tin. Bake in a moderate oven for 50 minutes.

N.B.—If hard mutton dripping is used, it may be slightly warmed to make it easier to rub in.

Economical Pastry (serves four)

1 oz. cooking fat
5 oz. plain flour and
2½ level teaspoons baking
powder or

5 oz. self-raising flour
½ level teaspoon salt
Milk to mix—about 4 tablespoons

Rub the fat into the flour, baking powder if used, and salt. Mix to a soft scone dough with the milk. Roll out and use in place of pastry for meat or fruit pies. Bake in a hot oven.

Potato Suet Pastry (serves four)

8 oz. plain flour and
4 level teaspoons baking
powder or
8 oz. self-raising flour

½ level teaspoon salt
2 oz. suet or other fat
2 oz. grated raw potato
Water to mix

Mix together the flour, baking powder if used, and the salt. Mix in the suet and potato. If other fat is used, rub it into the flour. Mix to a stiff dough with water. Use for meat puddings, fruit puddings, suet roll, dumplings or in any recipe using suet pastry.

Scones without Fat

8 oz. plain flour and
4 level teaspoons baking
powder or
8 oz. self-raising flour

½ level teaspoon salt
Approx. 6 tablespoons milk
or water to mix

Mix the flour, baking powder if used, and salt together. Mix to a soft dough with the milk or water, roll out to ½" thick and cut into rounds. Bake in a hot oven for 10-15 minutes. Alternatively, the scones may be cooked for 20-25 minutes on a girdle, or in a thick frying pan or on an electric hot-plate. Serve hot.

Dumplings

This mixture may also be used for dumplings. Shape the dough into small balls and drop into boiling liquid (soup, stew, fruit juice, etc.). Boil for 15-20 minutes.

SANDWICH FILLINGS

With these recipes there is no need to spread the bread with butter or margarine.

Savoury Leek Spread

2 oz. dripping
1 level tablespoon finely chopped leek
1 level teaspoon vegetable or meat extract

3 teaspoons of a Worcester sauce
Pepper and salt to taste

Slightly melt the dripping and beat well. Add the other ingredients and beat again.

Fish and Cabbage Spread

4 oz. pilchards or sardines
4 oz. finely shredded cabbage
1 level tablespoon chopped parsley

1 tablespoon vinegar
1 level teaspoon mustard
2 level teaspoons salt

Mix all ingredients together, mixing in some of the liquor from the fish. Beat well and use as a filling for scones, rolls or sandwiches.

Potted Cheese

1 level tablespoon flour
6 tablespoons water
2 oz. cheese, grated

1 oz. margarine
½ level teaspoon salt
Pinch of pepper

Blend the flour with the water and bring to the boil, stirring all the time; boil gently for 5 minutes. Add the cheese, margarine and seasoning and mix well. Allow to cool.

If liked, a little tomato sauce or meat extract can be added to the mixture.

Sweet Spread

1 oz. margarine
1 level dessertspoon syrup

1 tablespoon strong coffee
3 level dessertspoons cocoa

Mix well and spread on bread.

Revised and Reprinted
April, 1948.   84123402

Pye. Ltd. 51-3571.

ISSUED BY THE
MINISTRY OF FOOD

EVERY MOTHER AND
MOTHER-TO-BE SHOULD
READ THIS

EXTRAS

or the Expectant Mother

AND FOR CHILDREN UNDER 5

A word of advice to all expectant mothers

★ ★ ★

Once you have got a certificate from your doctor (or midwife, or health visitor) entitling you to a green ration book (in addition to your own buff book), the Government is anxious that you should make full use of the extras to which the green ration book entitles you.

It's important to remember that the life of a child starts nine months before birth. For these nine months the child lives on the mother, drawing food and fluid from her tissues. So, you see, you must begin *now* caring for the health of your baby by caring for yourself. And that means taking the extra nourishment you must have if your child is to be healthy and strong at birth.

The extras shown on the opposite page are all *needed* by the expectant mother. You shouldn't miss any one of them. Milk, eggs, meat, orange juice, vitamin tablets — these supply elements your body must have to feed the growing child, and they are made available by the Government specially for every mother-to-be. Be sure also to take up your full share of the ordinary rations.

If you visit your doctor or clinic regularly and follow the advice given, and take the extra food and vitamin supplements provided for you, you are doing all you can to ensure the health of your child.

ALL THESE **EXTRAS** ARE AVAILABLE FOR THE EXPECTANT MOTHER
in addition to her ordinary rations

Milk — a pint a day. You can get this at 1½d. per pint, or entirely free, if your income is below a certain limit — the Food Office will tell you.

Eggs. One shell egg at each allocation, on the green ration book.

Dried Egg. One packet every 8 weeks, free of points, on the green ration book.

Meat. A half ration on the green book.

Concentrated Orange Juice (containing vitamin C) — made from the juice of fresh oranges. Take a tablespoonful of orange juice in water every day.

A 6-oz. bottle of orange juice (containing the juice of 12 oranges) costs 5d. If you are eligible for free milk you will get your orange juice free as well.

Vitamin A and D tablets: These chocolate-coated tablets are rich in vitamins A and D, and contain calcium too. Take one tablet every day. If you like cod liver oil you can have that instead.

Vitamin A and D tablets or cod liver oil are supplied to you *free*, whatever your income.

Special coupons are provided at the back of the green ration book for orange juice and cod liver oil. Use the cod liver oil coupons for vitamin A and D tablets, if you prefer these.

Orange juice, vitamin A and D tablets, and cod liver oil are obtainable from local Food Offices, ante-natal clinics, Maternity and Child Welfare Centres, or other distribution centres. You can get a list of these at your Food Office.

Clothing coupons. You will be given 70 blue clothing coupons for the baby's clothes.

EVERY CHILD UNDER 5 GETS THESE
EXTRAS

MILK. Every child under 5 — that is, every child with a green ration book — is entitled to 7 pints of milk a week — at 1½d. a pint, or free — according to the income of the parents.

The mother of a baby under 12 months is also entitled to 7 pints of milk a week — at the ordinary price. If she is breast-feeding her baby she should take the whole of the 14 pints herself. If breast-feeding is not possible, or when weaning has begun, the milk should be given to the baby as advised by the doctor or the clinic.

National Dried Milk can be had in place of liquid milk for babies up to two years of age. The Food Office or Welfare Centre will tell you how to get this.

Eggs. All babies from 6 months to 2 years old can have fresh eggs at the rate of 3 a week. When the baby is 6 months old take the green ration book to the Food Office and get a special authorization for eggs.

Eggs are more digestible for babies when lightly boiled or coddled. "Coddled" means broken into a cup and cooked by standing the cup in a pan of boiling water for 3 or 4 minutes till the egg is set.

Dried Eggs. From birth to 5 years, every baby is entitled to a packet of dried eggs every 8 weeks, free of points.

Orange Juice. Every baby needs orange juice, which contains vitamin C, to ensure the health of the teeth and gums. Vitamin C also helps to keep the child in good all-round health.

Cod liver oil. Cod liver oil contains vitamins A and D, which are essential for building sound, healthy bones and teeth and for keeping the child resistant to infections.

Instructions for giving orange juice and cod liver oil are on the bottles. *Do not mix either cod liver oil or orange juice with the bottle feed.* And don't mix orange juice with hot water; it destroys the vitamin C. If you want to mix the orange juice with boiled water, let the water cool first.

Every child should have orange juice and cod liver oil regularly every day, without fail — summer and winter — until the age of 5.

Why Expectant Mothers need Orange Juice and Vitamin A and D tablets
EVERY DAY

Before your child is born, and 'r child is drawing nourishment from your 'irishme' is essential that you keep your body supplied with everything it needs for full health. Remember that you are doing a big job ! Your baby is dependent on you, and you alone, and you *must* see to it that you are equal to the task. The healthier you are, the healthier your child will be.

But there's another point to remember, and that is that if you neglect yourself now *you* will suffer later — even more than your child. An unborn child takes everything it needs from its mother, and if the mother does not make good what the child takes away, she will pay for it afterwards. General tiredness and poor health, back-ache, sore feet, decaying teeth — are often due solely to the mother failing to take essential food-stuffs during pregnancy.

Orange juice is rich in vitamin C — known as the "fresh fruit" vitamin. While fresh fruit is still not plentiful in the shops, orange juice is made available by the Government for expectant mothers. Vitamin C has a wonderful "toning-up"

effect on the health; also, it helps to keep the gums firm and healthy and the skin in good condition. The body needs vitamin C *every day*, and a tablespoonful of orange juice (taken in water) will give you all you need of this vitamin and make good any deficiencies caused by shortage of fruit.

Vitamins A and D, and calcium, are very important too for the expectant mother. Vitamins A and D are necessary for normal growth, for protecting the health of the body tissues and for the formation of bones and teeth. Calcium is essential for healthy bone structure and for sound teeth. Normally, you should get sufficient of these vitamins from such foods as butter, milk, egg-yolk and certain kinds of fish. To ensure that you do not go short of these now, the Government has provided concentrated tablets of vitamin A and D, with added calcium. You should take one tablet every day.

Don't let anything interfere with your taking your orange juice and vitamin tablets regularly. It may seem a trouble collecting them, but you will be amply repaid by giving this first importance.

WHAT TO DO WHEN BABY IS BORN

The baby's birth should be registered with the Registrar of births, as soon as possible. The Registrar will give you a form which you must take to the National Registration Officer, at the Food Office, where you will get an Identity Card for the baby, and the Green Ration Book, which you held before baby was born, will be altered to enable you to get the full range of rations. You will also get a clothing book and an extra soap ration for 12 months.

Take your own Buff Ration Book with you so that you can get the extra 7 pints of milk each week.

PLEASE BRING YOUR EMPTY BOTTLES WHEN YOU COLLECT YOUR NEXT SUPPLIES OF ORANGE JUICE OR COD LIVER OIL

ISSUED BY THE MINISTRY OF FOOD AND MINISTRY OF HEALTH

September 1946 51-2556-Gc.   64104809

COOKERY CONVERSION TABLES

Oven Temperatures

FAHRENHEIT	CELSCIUS	GAS MARK
230	110	$^1/_4$
250	120	$^1/_2$
265	130	1
285	140	1
300	150	2
320	160	3
340	170	4
355	180	4
375	190	5
390	200	6
410	210	6
430	220	7
445	230	8
460	240	9
480	250	9

Weights and Measures

Millilitres	Fluid Ounces	Cups	Teaspoons	Tablespoons
15ml	1/2 fl. oz		3	1
30 ml	1 fl. oz		6	2
56 ml	2 fl. oz		12	4
85 ml	3 fl. oz			6
115 ml	4 fl. oz	1/2		8
142 ml	5 fl. oz			10
170 ml	6 fl. oz	3/4		12
200 ml	7 fl. oz			14
230 ml	8 fl. oz	1		16
460 ml	16 fl. oz	2		32